D1505385

DISCARD

Ferrell v. Dallas I.S.D.

Hairstyles in Schools

Karen L. Trespacz

Landmark Supreme Court Cases

Enslow Publishers, Inc.

44 Fadem Road   PO Box 38
Box 699   Aldershot
Springfield, NJ 07081   Hants GU12 6BP
USA   UK

Library of Congress Cataloging-in-Publication Data

Trespacz, Karen L.
    Ferrell v. Dallas I.S.D. : hairstyles in schools / Karen L. Trespacz.
        p. cm. — (Landmark Supreme Court cases)
    Includes bibliographical references and index.
        Summary: Discusses the case in which three students in the Dallas
Independent School District were suspended from school in 1966
because of their hairstyles.
    ISBN 0-7660-1054-6
    1. Ferrell, L.W.—Trials, litigation, etc.—Juvenile literature.
2. Dallas Independent School District (Tex.)—Trials, litigation,
etc.—Juvenile literature. 3. Student suspension—Law and
legislation—Texas—Juvenile literature. [1. Ferrell, L. W.—
Trials, litigation, etc. 2. Dallas Independent School District
(Tex.) 3. Student suspension.] I. Title II. Series
KF228.F44T74   1998
344.764'0793—dc21   97-28930
                                                          CIP
                                                           AC

Printed in the United States of America

10 9 8 7 6 5 4 3 2

Photo Credits: Courtesy of John M.W. Lancaster, p. 111; Harris and Ewing,
Collection of the Supreme Court of the United States, p. 99; Hessler Studios,
Collection of the Supreme Court of the United States, p. 95; Library of Congress,
pp. 9, 12, 18, 23, 28, 40, 69, 74, 105; National Archives, pp. 21, 44, 48, 53, 58,
86, 90, 96.

Cover Photo: The Picture Cube

Contents

Publisher's Note

Thousands of cases are sent to the Supreme Court each year for consideration. Only a very small percentage of those is ever actually considered by the Court, however. This case is one that the Supreme Court chose *not* to hear. We have included it in our Landmark Supreme Court Case series because it deals with the important issue of rights for students in schools. Despite the fact that it was never actually heard by the Justices of the Supreme Court, the publisher feels it is an interesting and relevant case for our readers.

Acknowledgments

The author would like to thank the following people for their patience and kind assistance; without their help, this book would not have been possible:

Pat Anderson, Lisa Blumberg, Herbert Hooks, the Lancaster family (Robin, John, Willie, and Larom), Marjorie Millen, Elyse Plosky, Jackie Pryor, Eric Russman, Barbara Rust, Jennifer Trespacz, and Mr. & Mrs. Dudley Watkins.

A special note of thanks also goes to Jim Cohen and to Dick Baxter for teaching me how to write.

1

Hairstyle Keeps Students Out of School

Phil, Steve, and Paul were seventeen and they felt that their rock band, Sounds Unlimited, could be a real success.[1] They had been playing as a group with their friends, Ronnie and Chuck, for about a year and a half when a conflict occurred. Steve and Phil played electric guitar. Paul had started to play organ in the group about six months before. Chuck played the drums.

They had even signed a contract with an agent that August. They called him "Alexander the Great," although his real name was Kent Alexander. The contract—which their parents signed, too—required their agent to help them become successful as a rock group. The contract also required the boys to do certain things. One of the requirements was that they wear their hair long, like the members of the rock group the Beatles. (See photo on page 9.) At the time the boys signed their contract, the Beatles were a very new band. Their look was very exciting. It was 1966, only two years after the Beatles had first come to the United States.

All of the boys already had long hair, so growing it to satisfy their contractual obligations would not be an issue. As Paul's mother would later describe his hair to the judge, "Paul's hair does not come to his eyebrows in the front, it comes maybe an inch and a half away from it and about half over his ears and it is long in the back and it's not down below his collar."[2] Steve's mother described his hair this way, "It's over his eyes, you can see the ear lobe below it, it is down on the neck somewhat, however, it doesn't curl up in the back, it hangs over the forehead to his eyebrows. . . ."[3] The judge himself later said of Phil's hair:

> if hanging straight forward, would come below his eyebrows, but [it] is combed and turned to the side so as to be a very short distance above his eyebrows. The hair extends down to the ear lobe on the side and to the collar in the back.[4]

The problem was that Phil, Steve, and Paul were supposed to start their senior year at W. W. Samuell High School (a public school) soon and they might not be allowed to attend school with their hair that long. The school's concern about long hair was something the boys already knew about when they signed the contract. Paul had his hair trimmed that summer in order to get into summer school. Steve had been told more than once the year before to have his hair trimmed before he came back to school. Obviously, the school's concern about hair had not gone away.

About a week before school started, Paul's friend Mike asked Paul to go with him to school to check his school schedule. The Dean of Girls, Mrs. Gilbert, happened to be in the office while they were there. Mike pointed to Paul and asked Mrs. Gilbert if Paul and the others in the rock group could get in with their hair like that. No, Mrs. Gilbert replied, they would have to go through Mr. Lanham (the principal) or Mr. Matthews (the assistant principal) to be admitted.[5] If Paul's hair was a problem, Phil and Steve were sure to have a problem because Paul's hair was the shortest of the three.

The issue was fresh in the boys' minds when, on Thursday evening, September 1, 1966, they got together for an "A & R," arrangement and recording session.[6] As Mr. Alexander later explained,

> We had some professional equipment with our company on this and the practice session was at one of the boys' houses. What we do is go over a song, record it and play it back and listen to the mistakes and then

7

work out the mistakes. This is the same thing as working up a song."[7]

After the session was over and while the technical people were loading up their equipment, Paul told Mr. Alexander what Mrs. Gilbert had said. As Mr. Alexander later reported, "This became of utmost concern to me because of the business I'm in and in the regard that I have for the boys as far as personality is concerned."[8]

Of course, it was of concern to the boys, too; they wanted to finish their last year in high school and they also wanted to be successful rock musicians.[9] Paul asked Mr. Alexander to talk to the school principal to see whether they could go to school without having to cut their hair.

The Conflict

On Tuesday, September 6, the night before school opened, Mr. Alexander called Principal Lanham at home. Alexander explained to the principal that he had a contract with the boys. He had invested a significant amount of money in their rock group, and long hair was very important to the success of the group.

Principal Lanham was an experienced, hardworking, and dedicated professional educator. How much money students made on their own time was not his concern;

helping them get a good public education was. School opening was a busier time than usual. W. W. Samuell High was a large school; at the time it had over twenty-four hundred students. Yet here he was being called at home, at one of the busiest times of the year, on the night before a very big day, by someone who was not a parent, about hair.

Without having seen the boys, Principal Lanham could not say whether their hair was a problem or not.

The Beatles created a revolution in American music—and American hairstyles—in the 1960s. This 1964 picture of the Beatles shows the hairstyle that Phil, Paul, and Steve were required to have under their contract with their agent.

He tried to describe to Alexander the way the school handled any kind of student appearance that would distract from the operation of the school. As Mr. Lanham later described the conversation:

> But he kept bringing it up about the boys and about the matter about the money, the amount of money they could make, and I said, "They can make all the money they can as long as it does not interfere with the matter of their entering high school." I tried to explain to him and he wasn't interested so I told him I could not continue the conversation and that I could not talk to him about the situation, that I would only talk to the parents and to the students. But he would not stop and he kept on and got to talking about this money and I tried to explain to him over and over and I finally hung up on him.[10]

Mr. Lanham found the call very frustrating. He also felt that the call was a challenge to his authority.[11]

The following morning, rather than go to their homerooms as usual, the three boys went to meet with Principal Lanham in his office. They met at the school about 8:30 A.M. with Phil's mother. Steve's mother got there a few minutes later and joined them in the school lobby. Mr. Alexander was there, too. Paul's father had given him authority to speak because Paul's father could not be at the meeting.

They waited about forty-five minutes to see the principal. Then Assistant Principal Matthews came out to meet them and usher them into the principal's office.

Then Matthews discovered that Alexander was not a parent but was the agent who had called the principal the night before. Matthews became angry and said, "We have nothing to talk to you about. You took up about thirty minutes of Mr. Lanham's time yesterday and we told you not to come back here."[12] Matthews then asked Alexander to leave.

Alexander headed for the telephone while the others went to the office. When Principal Lanham came out of his office to greet them, Alexander turned around to join the group. Again Alexander was asked to leave. On his way out, he turned to give the boys last-minute instructions. That is when the principal and the assistant principal got on either side of him and escorted him out of the school building.

What were those last-minute instructions? Different people thought they heard different things. Principal Lanham thought he heard Alexander say something along the lines of "You know what I told you to do."[13] Paul thought he heard the agent say something much less ominous such as, "You boys keep a cool head and be respectable."[14]

There was not going to be agreement at the meeting they held in the principal's office, either. Principal Lanham told them that if they could find a way to wear their hair so that the length would not be extremely noticeable, it would be all right with him. He had to maintain rules about student appearance, however, because of the way it affected behavior.

The boys and the parents asked where the rule came from, "Is it a city rule? Is it a school administration rule? What rule is it? Where is it written?"[15] "At times," Steve's mother later said, "it appeared to be his decision and at other times it appeared to be the decision of the school administration . . . but it was never made clear what rule was being violated."[16]

Look at the short hair on all the male students in this 1966 picture. This is what the principal was used to seeing in the halls of his school. In 1966, people were upset with long hair on males.

In the end, the boys said that they would not cut their hair because they were under contract with Mr. Alexander. Principal Lanham said that Phil and Steve could not enroll until their hair was trimmed. Paul, whose hair had not yet grown out from his summer school trim, could enroll that day.

The Response

All three boys left the school after the meeting ended, around 9:45 A.M. As they walked out of the school, they were met by a reporter from the *Times Herald* newspaper. Then radio and television reporters started to arrive. Half an hour after the boys had left the principal's office, they held a press conference on the sidewalk at one corner of the school grounds.

How did the press know the results of the conversation in the principal's office so soon after it happened? Kent Alexander had called them. He was thorough about it, too; he had called at least seven places—newspapers, radio stations, and television stations—although not all of them came.

After the press conference the boys continued trying to re-enter school. That afternoon they went to the general administration building for the Dallas Independent School District to try to see the super-intendent. (The superintendent was the head of the whole school district, under the board of education.) They met the assistant superintendent on the steps of the building. He told them that the superintendent was not in the building. It would be about two weeks before they could see him. The assistant superintendent also told them that the school had no written policy about long hair and that principals made their own hair rules.

The next day, the boys went back to W. W. Samuell High School and were again refused admittance. They then went to seven other high schools, trying to find one that would admit them. They had no success.

Later that afternoon they wrote a song in protest, "Keep Your Hands Off of It," about being kept out of school by a principal because of long hair. Mr. Alexander made the arrangements for them to go to a recording studio to record it. The session started around 8 P.M. and ended after midnight. Right after they recorded the master, they took it across the hall to have demos (demonstration copies) made. Then, they took a demo to a radio station. It was first aired that Friday morning. Over the next few weeks, it was played by several radio stations and at least one television station. Principal Lanham took the song personally.[17]

The day the song first aired, the boys went back to W. W. Samuell High to talk to Principal Lanham about getting a transfer to another school. He could not take their transfer applications because school policy did not permit transfers during the few weeks around school opening. It was during that conversation that Steve apologized to Principal Lanham for the song.

Phil, Steve, and Paul went back to W. W. Samuell High one last time to try to get in, the following Tuesday, September 13. At that point, because Paul's hair had grown during the course of the week, Principal Lanham refused to enroll any of the boys.

The Question

The boys had tried several different ways to get permission to go to high school and keep their hairstyle, too. Their agent had called the principal to talk to him. They had talked to the principal in his office with their parents. They had tried to enter seven other high schools. They had tried to see the superintendent. They had made one final plea to their own principal. But still they could not get in without cutting their hair. What would they do now?

2

Part of a Bigger Picture

Conflict over hairstyles did not start with Phil, Steve, and Paul; hairstyle conflicts have been around for thousands of years. In biblical times, a war started between the Israelites and the Ammonites because the Ammonite king ordered the beards shaved off King David's messengers.[1] Later, when the shorthaired Romans conquered the longhaired people of Gaul, Caesar ordered his troops to cut the conquered men's hair. William the Conqueror did much the same thing when he conquered Great Britain; he forced a number of his new British subjects to cut their hair and to shave. In France during the 1500s, some French judges would not let bearded men bring a lawsuit until the men shaved. Joseph Palmer, a Massachusetts man, went through an amazing amount of harassment in the

1800s for wearing a beard; he was even jailed for over a year.[2]

People have also argued over women's styles. In the early 1920s, there was a lot of conflict over women with short hair. "Bobbed hair" was what the short hairstyle was called; it was preached against as a symbol of everything that was wrong with America in those days. Some men divorced their wives because their wives cut their hair. Some husbands refused to shave until their wives let their hair grow long again. Women were fired from their jobs because they had bobbed hair.[3]

The conflict over long hair that included Phil, Steve, and Paul was part of a broader conflict that reached around the world. There were crackdowns on longerhaired young men in Argentina, Austria, Brazil, Bulgaria, Chile, China, Czechoslovakia, Hong Kong, Indonesia, Mexico, Singapore, and Thailand. In some of those countries, men with long hair were kept out altogether, or if they were already there, arrested and given a haircut. In Vietnam, haircuts were forced on more than fourteen hundred young men during three weeks in 1970.[4]

Civil Rights

Conflict over hair was not the only conflict happening in the 1960s, nor was it the only conflict that affected

Hair has been so important to people that they have tried all kinds of things down through the ages to get the look they wanted. This woman appears to be getting a permanent wave.

Steve, Phil, and Paul. Among the many conflicts in those days was a conflict over civil rights, the movement to give black Americans the same rights as white Americans.

There were many civil rights demonstrations in the late 1950s and early 1960s. One of the most famous civil rights demonstrations happened in August 1963. The Reverend Martin Luther King, Jr., led approximately two hundred thousand people in a march on Washington, D.C. He gave voice to their hopes and visions in his inspiring "I Have a Dream" speech. The federal Civil Rights Act was enacted less than a year later, in July 1964. It prohibited racial discrimination on the job, in public places, in government-owned facilities, and in programs receiving federal funds.[5]

How did the civil rights conflict affect the boys? First and foremost, it affected the relationship between schools and students. Prior to the civil rights movement, it had not been unusual for school systems to have separate schools for whites and blacks. "Separate but equal" was the idea, but it did not work. Schools for white students had better buildings, books, and equipment than schools for black students. In 1954, the United States Supreme Court decided in the *Brown* v. *Board of Education* case that "separate" meant "unequal" and, therefore, public schools systems had to admit both blacks and whites to their schools.[6] Teaching students of all races in the same schools was called integration. However, it took many years for integration to be instituted in this country.

This Court ruling was strengthened by passage of the 1964 Civil Rights Act. Public schools were established by the government and many (if not all) received federal funds. Because of this, public school systems were subject to the act's requirement to avoid discrimination.

The boys' public school district was required to integrate, too. On the same day that the boys first tried to get into school, approximately 40 percent of the Dallas Independent School District schools became integrated for the first time. Obviously, the district superintendent had a lot of things on his mind that day.

The civil rights movement was centered on the idea that all citizens should be treated equally. The boys would use this argument in federal court. They claimed they were being discriminated against because of their long hair. They also felt that keeping them out of school violated the Civil Rights Act.

Rock Music

The boys were also affected by the changes going on in rock music. The "British Invasion" had hit America. It

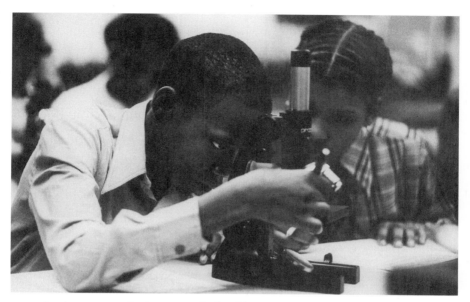

Students cannot be kept out of school because of their skin color. Do you think it would be fair to keep these students out of school because of their hairstyles?

started with the Beatles, and included such rock bands as the Rolling Stones, The Who, and The Kinks. It was because the Beatles look was so popular that the boys were required by contract to wear their hair long. (Ironically, while American teenagers were going wild for the music of the Beatles and other British rock groups, that music was not fundamentally British; it had its roots in the rhythm and blues of African-American performers in the United States. The British groups were strongly influenced by such performers as Little Richard, Bo Diddley, and Chuck Berry.)[7]

Steve, Phil, and Paul were most likely also affected by the enthusiasm and hope common among teenage musicians then. Contests were being held for teenage rock groups. The winners could get professional recording contracts. Many students in those days started playing instruments and formed rock groups with the hope of making it big. Phil, Paul, and Steve had achieved a measure of success that many other student rock groups must have envied. Their song, "Keep Your Hands Off of It," had been played repeatedly on the radio and copies of it were sold in stores.

But it is unlikely that the boys made a great deal of money from their record; a lot of other people had to be paid first. After the boys had written their song, their agent made arrangements with a recording studio to have the song recorded. As the agent later reported, "I merely made a phone call and said this is Kent Alexander of National Artist and I would like to reserve the studio at 8:00. . . ."[8] The studio was paid for use of its recording room and equipment, so that the master tape could be made. A recording company was then paid to make ten demonstration copies from the master. The demos were taken to radio stations with the request that they be played on the air.

After that, the boys' agent made arrangements for a record producing company to make 1,000 "single" records. (A single record had just one song on each side.) Of the 1,000 records, 700 went to a distributing company. The boys' agent distributed 150, and 150 were kept for use as promotional copies, for example, as giveaways at various events.

The distributing company did not buy the records it got, however. The boys' agent testified that the boys would not be paid anything until the distributing company got someone else to buy the records.

This is a 1967 picture of a teenage rock group at a teen club. The boys' rock group may have looked like this.

So far many people had been paid—the studio, the company that made the demos, the company that made the records, and possibly, the distributing company. When would the boys be paid?

As their agent explained it, every time the song was played on the radio, and every time the record was sold, money would be owed to the boys. It would be a specific amount of money each time the song was played, and a percentage of the sale price for each record that was sold. That percentage for Phil, Paul, and Steve was 5 percent. Singles at that time were selling for about one dollar per record. So the boys would earn about five cents for every record sold. Well, almost. The money, which was paid either every three months or every six months, was actually paid to their agent. Under the contract that the boys signed, their agent kept some of the money and gave the rest to the boys.

So how much did the agent keep? It is not clear because he explained the arrangement he had with the boys two different ways in court. However, using the method that would give the most money to the boys, even if all 1,000 records were sold, each boy would get less than eight dollars.

3

The Boys Go to Court

The boys decided to bring a lawsuit against their principal and their high school. They had to get past several hurdles, however, before they could do that. They had to get past issues of law—who could sue, and what they wanted to happen if they won.

Because these issues can get complicated, most people hire lawyers to help them. It was no different for the boys; Attorneys Herbert L. Hooks and Dan Gibbs were hired to help them bring their lawsuit to court. While the lawyers did all the legal work, the lawsuit still belonged to the boys; the boys were the ones with the conflict. So the case is presented from the point of view of the people most involved—Phil, Paul, and Steve.

Which Law?

The boys could not sue simply because they disagreed with what the principal did. They had to show that the principal and the school had done something that was against the law.

One of the first places to look for possible laws that had been broken would be the statute books. These are the books that recite the laws that were passed either by state lawmakers or by Congress. Another place to look would be the United States Constitution and the Texas constitution. (Constitutions are the blueprints that guide lawmakers in passing laws. If lawmakers passed a law that was in conflict with either the United States Constitution or that of Texas, and if someone took that conflict to court, the court could declare the law unconstitutional and the law would have no validity.)

Looking at the state law books, the boys found that the Texas state constitution provided for the establishment of free public schools in Texas.[1] Texas state lawmakers had passed a law that said:

> The board of school trustees of any . . . independent or common school district shall admit to the benefits of the public schools any person over six and not over twenty-one years old at the beginning of the scholastic year. . . .[2]

Texas laws also provided that the trustees of public

schools "may suspend from the privileges of schools any pupil found guilty of incorrigible conduct. . . ."[3] (Incorrigible conduct means behavior that is very bad, with no possibility it will improve.)

Looking at the laws of the United States, the boys found that the idea of "equal rights for all" was based on the Fourteenth Amendment to the United States Constitution, particularly the part that says states must not deny to any person the equal protection of the law. The boys then found that under the Civil Rights Act, people who feel that they have been treated unequally can sue.

But the boys still had to look in one more place— the books that report court decisions. It was not enough to see the words in the laws, they also needed to see how the courts interpreted them. (This is called "case law.")

To give a civil rights example, does the Fourteenth Amendment's guarantee of equal protection under the law mean that there can be separate schools for blacks and whites? In 1896, the United States Supreme Court in *Plessy* v. *Ferguson* decided that it was lawful to separate whites and blacks as long as the places they could go were equal.[4] So separate schools were legal. Then in 1954, when it had become clear that "separate" produced situations that were very unequal, the United States Supreme Court in *Brown* v. *Board of Education* reversed itself and decided that separate schools were prohibited by the Fourteenth Amendment.[5] So separate schools became illegal. The words of the Fourteenth Amendment did not change. The way the Court interpreted those words did, however.

Courts are supposed to apply laws the same way under the same circumstances. This is called precedent. If the boys had found cases that described conflicts like theirs and their side had won, they could argue to the court that those cases were setting a precedent and they

Where do laws come from? Sometimes they come from places like this. This is a 1966 picture of the room where the Texas House of Representatives met to vote on proposed laws.

should win, too. Here is where the boys ran into a problem. They found two cases that suggested that students should *not* be able to sue in situations like theirs; one case in particular suggested that students could only sue under the Civil Rights Act if the students faced *racial* discrimination. But the boys' conflict was about hair; it was not about race. Did this mean that they could not go to federal court? Maybe. What the boys had to do was try to distinguish their case from the ones they found. They would have to show that their circumstances were different enough from the circumstances in the other cases so that their result should be different, too.

Which Court?

In which court should the boys sue? Just as there are state laws and federal laws, there are state courts and federal courts. There are a number of other courts, too, like municipal courts, small claims courts, tax courts, and military courts. Only courts that had the authority to decide about the laws the boys were using—courts that had jurisdiction—would let them present their case.

Since the boys were basing their argument on a federal law, they prepared to sue in federal court. A court will often not hear a suit against a governmental agency until that agency has finally decided what it will do. In lawyers' terms, a court will not accept jurisdiction until the matter is "ripe." The boys filed suit less than a week after they were denied enrollment. Was the school's decision final enough for a court to hear the case?

Who Sues?

Did the boys have a right to sue? That would depend on whether they had "standing," that is, whether they were the right people to bring the case. To have standing, they would have to be directly involved in the conflict. For example, their agent could not have sued, even though he told the local newspaper that he was going to.[6] The agent did not have standing; a conflict about school admission is between the school and the students (and their parents).

In this case, the boys were directly involved, but they were not old enough to bring suit on their own. So their parents sued on their behalf.

What Would They Ask For?

The boys had found laws to support their case, they had picked a court, and their parents had standing to sue for them. What would they sue for? In order to bring a lawsuit, they had to tell the court not only what the other side did wrong, but also what they wanted to happen if they won. In the language lawyers use, they had to say what "remedy" they were looking for.

There are different kinds of remedies a court can grant. For example, a court can order the losing side to pay a certain amount of money to the winning side or can order the losing side to give something back. In this case, the boys asked the court to order the principal to allow them to attend school with their long hairstyles.

Lawsuits can take years. What would happen to the boys in the meantime? For example, even if the courts eventually decided that the boys were right and they could go to school with long hair, by the time they enrolled, all of their friends might have graduated.

Fortunately, there are legal tools to deal with problems like this. The first is a temporary restraining order. That document could order the principal and the school to let the boys back in immediately, but it would only last a short while. A temporary restraining order is only intended to stop what may be a harmful situation until a court can hear arguments about the situation.

The second legal tool is a temporary injunction. A temporary injunction would order the principal and the school to let the boys go to school until the whole lawsuit process was over (or until they graduated, which-ever came first). Because the temporary injunction could last for such a long time, however, the boys had to convince the federal court judge that they had a good chance of winning before the court would grant one.

The boys asked for both. They won the temporary restraining order, and on September 13, the federal district court ordered Principal Lanham to let the boys attend high school. At the same time, the court set a hearing date for less than two weeks later. At the hearing, both sides would present arguments so the court could decide whether to accept the case and, if accepted, whether to grant the boys' request for a temporary injunction.

The Hearing Starts

The hearing started on Thursday, September 22, 1966, before the Honorable William M. Taylor, United States District Judge, in the United States District Court for the Northern District of Texas, Dallas Division.

Hearings generally start with the lawyers from each side making opening statements, summarizing why the judge should agree with them. The boys' parents were the plaintiffs, the ones who filed the lawsuit. Because of this, their attorney, Herbert L. Hooks, was first to present his case.

The pressure was on Hooks. If he could not convince the judge to hear the case, then the boys would be thrown out of school again. All of the people who had come to the court for the hearing—all three boys, their parents, and the boys' friends—would have to go home without being able to say anything.

Hooks began by tackling the hardest part first. He tried to distinguish the cases that said students should not be allowed into federal court from this case. He then argued that the federal Civil Rights Act of 1964 and the Fourteenth Amendment to the United States Constitution prohibited more than racial discrimination. They should be understood to prohibit discrimination against anyone.

Next, Hooks pointed out that the boys had a right to equal access to public education under federal law. They also had a right to a free public education under Texas law. Having tried to show that the boys' legal arguments were strong, Hooks then tried to show that the legal arguments on the other side were weak. In the school's written response to the lawsuit, the school had said that the matter was "frivolous" and, therefore, not important enough for a federal court to hear. But Hooks argued that, on the contrary, this was important. This was a matter as serious as a government official's keeping citizens from an education that was theirs under both federal and state law. If there was anything frivolous at all about the case, he argued, it was the reason the principal used to keep the boys from getting their education—their hairstyle. If hairstyles were not that important, then they were not serious enough to keep three students out of school.

Finally, Herbert Hooks went back to federal and state law and summed up why this case should be heard by the federal court and why the boys had a winning argument. Then, it was the other side's turn.

WHO'S WHO

On the Boys' Side

The Boys:
- Phillip Ferrell
- Paul Jarvis
- Stephen Webb

The Boys' Attorneys:
- Attorney Herbert L. Hooks
- Attorney Dan Gibbs

On the School's Side

The Defendants:
- W. S. Lanham—the principal for the boys' high school
- W. T. White—the district superintendent
- Dallas Independent School District—the public school system that included W. W. Samuell High School, the boys' school.

The Defense Attorneys:
- Attorney Franklin L. Spafford
- Attorney Warren Whitham

Attorney Warren Whitham was very brief. Herbert Hooks's argument had gone over twelve pages in the final hearing transcript. Whitham talked for a very short time, then stopped. He argued that there were not any real differences between the two earlier cases and this one. Those cases were controlling, he argued, so the boys' case should be dismissed. Now it was the judge's turn. What would he decide?

The judge decided not to decide. He pointed out that in one of those other two cases, the presiding judge had heard all the evidence before making his decision. So Judge Taylor decided that he should hear all of the evidence, too. That would help him determine whether his court had jurisdiction.

The boys had not won the war yet, but they had won a major battle. They could now present all the evidence they had to show that their argument was justifiable.

4

The Case for the Boys

The first witnesses were the two mothers who had met with Principal Lanham on the first day of school. The boys' parents were, after all, the named plaintiffs in the case. It would also be a good start to show that the adults most responsible for the boys' upbringing, their parents, thought the boys were doing the right thing. As Paul's mother said on the witness stand, "I felt Paul's hair was perfectly the right length to go to school. I didn't see anything wrong with it."[1]

Having set the stage, the boys' attorneys then brought on the leading opponent—Principal Lanham. It was a bold move, putting the principal on the witness stand even before letting the boys tell their story. But if they waited until the principal's own attorneys called him, his attorneys would ask questions that would try to make the principal sound as reasonable as possible. So the boys' attorneys would ask questions that would try to show that the principal's position was unreasonable. If they asked those questions first, maybe the judge's impression of the principal's side would be less favorable.

Attorney Herbert Hooks started his direct examination by exploring Principal Lanham's authority to make a decision about the boys' hairstyles. The school board gave principals the authority to govern student appearance. Appearance should not interfere with getting a public education. That meant that there was no specific rule that said "no Beatles hairstyles." It was up to each principal to decide what was acceptable.

> **Attorney Hooks:** In your opinion, did you feel that the boys in question and the style of their hair would cause a distraction or a disturbance in your school?
>
> **Principal Lanham:** Yes, sir.
>
> **Attorney Hooks:** In what respect?
>
> **Principal Lanham:** Well, anything that's unusual or out of the ordinary causes a distraction. We've worked with this problem for several years.[2]

Attorney Hooks asked why Paul, who had been allowed to enroll on the first day of school, had been kept out less than a week later.

> **Principal Lanham:** He had another week's growth and

his hair was approaching the length of the other two boys at that time.

Attorney Hooks: He had one week's growth to a point where in your opinion it would be a disturbing influence or a distraction in your school?

Principal Lanham: That's what I said.[3]

Hooks tried other approaches that would raise questions about the principal's decision. If pictures of longhaired men on the wall were not a distraction, how could longhaired students in the classroom be a distraction? Hooks asked about pictures of George Washington.

Attorney Hooks: Of course, we all know his hair was down at his shoulder?

Principal Lanham: He wasn't a high school student.[4]

Was the principal's decision a bad one because he had not taken into account the boys' obligation under their contract to keep their hair long?

Attorney Hooks: You didn't feel that any special consideration should be given to these boys in the application of your rule because they were trying to earn their expenses or trying to make money on the side?

Principal Lanham: I did not. That was brought out by the mother of one of them. If they had gotten special permission and nobody else had that permission, to me, that does violate democratic principles.[5]

But was the principal's decision really based on personal taste, and not on its effect on the school?

> **Attorney Hooks:** I take it you personally dislike the hairstyle?
>
> **Principal Lanham:** I don't care to answer that. That's a personal opinion and I don't see how it has anything to do with it. I might like you with glasses on or I might prefer you with glasses off, but I don't think that makes any difference and it is not going to make any difference in the operation of the school. I try to be as fair and as impartial as I know how.[6]

But was the principal's decision unreasonable in light of the fact that longer hair was getting more and more common?

> **Attorney Hooks:** Mr. Lanham, you don't feel because of movies and television and magazine and newspapers and teenagers frequently having their hair like that, your students are accustomed to this style and to them it is not distracting?
>
> **Principal Lanham:** Movies and television and that sort of thing are different surroundings from the matter of school and at school they are there to get an education, and we attempt to have the climate so they can get an education without too many distractions.[7]

Now it was time for the other side to cross-examine the witness. The school's lawyers, starting with Franklin Spafford, would ask questions to try to make the principal's decision sound as reasonable as possible. They started with the idea that maybe the conflict was not

Thomas Jefferson.

Read the descriptions of the boys' hair in Chapter 1. Do the descriptions seem to fit Thomas Jefferson's hair in this picture? If Thomas Jefferson could be president with long hair, why could Phil, Paul, and Steve not be students with long hair?

about enrolling in school at all; maybe the fuss was just part of a plan to get publicity for the boys' rock group.

Their questions and Principal Lanham's answers established the fact that of all the students in his high school, only these three came to see him rather than go to their homerooms. The boys had taken an active role in what happened. Their agent had also. The agent had called Principal Lanham the night before and was there with the boys at school that morning.

> **Attorney Spafford:** What did he say to the boys? Did he give them any instructions as to what they were to do in talking to you?
>
> **Principal Lanham:** He was in the hallway when I opened the door for the parents and the boys to go directly into my office and he started over to the door as they came along, and he said you boys do this and do that and I asked him to leave the building.
>
> **Attorney Spafford:** What did he say? Did you overhear what he said?
>
> **Principal Lanham:** He said, "You know what I told you to do," and so forth. I don't remember exactly but that's in effect what he said.[8]

How about the basis for the principal's decision? Were there actual problems connected to long hair?

> **Attorney Spafford:** How does it [long hair] affect the educational program?
>
> **Principal Lanham:** Well, in the matter of different types of disturbances for example, [in regard to] long

hair there are certain boys that will make it pretty hard on some of these youngsters and sometimes the language that they speak to them in the hallway—and we had an occasion where girls came to the office complaining about the language being used between some of these boys and another factor was that they challenged them to fight.

Judge Taylor: Is this language you mentioned what you would call, Mr. Lanham, obscene language that the girls were complaining about?

Principal Lanham: Yes.

Attorney Spafford: And were there fights or threatened fights?

Principal Lanham: There were a number of occasions.[9]

Later in the questioning, Judge Taylor came back to the effect hair could have in a school setting.

Judge Taylor: Just tell us how the long hair affects your management of the discipline and deportment and good order in school?

Principal Lanham: Well, I mentioned these incidents and there are others where some of the boys when they see a boy with long hair they will tell him that the girl's restroom is right down the hall. . . . We had a long hair boy . . . [who] wouldn't go to the boy's restroom until they left. We had other incidents where the boys would eat in the lunchroom only with the girls and never eat with the boys. We've had another case where a boy was running around with younger boys and not the boys of his age, and we had one boy that was a loner, so to speak, and he finally dropped out and joined the Navy. These are just some of the things that come to mind that have happened as a result of distractions in the school.[10]

Next, the point was made that the school does not discriminate against boys; it disciplines girls for appearance, too.

> **Attorney Spafford:** What other extremes in dress do you have to deal with?
>
> **Principal Lanham:** Sometimes we have problems with the girls and I don't do too much of that, I depend on the pupil personnel who is directly involved if the girls—there have been cases where they have been sent home to change their dress because there was too much exposed. We usually call the parents and there are other examples of too much make-up and long lashes.
>
> **Attorney Spafford:** False eyelashes?
>
> **Principal Lanham:** And paint and that sort of thing and they have been asked to remove some of them so that it would not be so conspicuous. They can't wear any type of dress, the girls are expected to wear dresses and not tight-fitting pants and they are supposed to wear shoes and not come around barefooted and I could go on with things like that. We feel like it's the school's responsibility to lead these young people and that dress has a very important effect on their school situation.[11]

Spafford closed the cross-examination with a series of questions to try to make the principal's case both cleanly and clearly, first about the importance of appearance.

Attorney Spafford: So, there is a direct correlation between behavior or discipline and dress?

Principal Lanham: That's been my experience down through the years in dealing with high school pupils.

Attorney Spafford: And is that the foundation for the requirement that the dress not be extreme?

Principal Lanham: That's right.

Then Spafford tried to make the point that the boys were not really serious about enrolling in school:

Attorney Spafford: Did they finally accept any of your offers to try to [resolve the matter] by just trimming the length of their hair?

Girls can wear long hair to school. Is it fair to tell boys they cannot?

Principal Lanham: None at all.[12]

Now it was the boys' turn again, so Herbert Hooks asked Principal Lanham more questions on redirect examination. Maybe the correlation between appearance and behavior was not as strong as it sounded on cross-examination.

> **Attorney Hooks:** What you're saying is that it's the effect of having long hair that causes a problem?
>
> **Principal Lanham:** That's kind of like the chicken and the egg.
>
> **Attorney Hooks:** Mr. Lanham, let me put it another way then, you do not really expect a young boy to have morale problems concerning conduct because he lets his hair grow long, do you?
>
> **Principal Lanham:** Yes, it actually happens.[13]

But what about the extent of the principal's control? The principal has a say about student appearance on school grounds, but what about rules that would affect students outside of school?

> **Attorney Hooks:** There's a great difference between hair and clothes, you can change clothes and you can't change your hair, isn't that right?
>
> **Principal Lanham:** Well, temporarily, their hair is not permanent because I've lost lots of mine. It is considered a part of their dress.
>
> **Attorney Hooks:** You don't try to control your students and their personal appearance when they are off

the school premises and the area of the school grounds?

Principal Lanham: No.

Attorney Hooks: You leave their freedom of taste and personal desires up to them and their parents when they are out of your sight or out of your control and authority?"

Principal Lanham: Yes.[14]

The boys had been in school since the temporary restraining order was granted on September 13; it was now September 22. Had there been any actual problems?

Principal Lanham: There's been no particular distraction.[15]

This was exactly the point that the boys wanted to make. But sometimes if you push on a point you like, you get something you don't like.

Attorney Hooks: I'm specifically asking you as to their learning, do you feel that you as an educator sincerely believe that they will learn less as a result of the length of their hair or the students around them will?

Principal Lanham: Well, it seems that this has happened in the case of these boys and in one particular case that I can think of where his grades dropped last year.

Attorney Hooks: Whose did?

Principal Lanham: Let's see, I think it was Steve.[16]

Just when it looked like there was a winning point

being made, the testimony took a turn for the worse for the boys. The judge called a fifteen-minute recess. Maybe there was another explanation for the drop in grades. If there was, the judge had to hear it right away before he concluded that the principal was right. When the court reconvened, the boys' other lawyer, Dan Gibbs, called Steve to the witness stand.

Attorney Gibbs: Do you have an explanation or can you tell us whether or not you were academically holding your grades up?

Steve: Well, my first three years of high school I was taking high academic English and math and last year my junior year . . . and during the summer before I was working thirty or forty hours a week. And at the first of school I went to the counselor and tried to explain my problem and that I would like to be taken out of high academic math because I was really having a problem with it and it was so hard and it was so hard at first I didn't see how I could do it and I begged and pleaded for her to take me out of it and she refused. And I was working thirty or forty hours a week and trying to go to school at the same time and it didn't mix too well and I failed a course at the end of the semester.

Attorney Gibbs: You failed one course last year?

Steve: Yes, sir, one course.

Attorney Gibbs: And that was high academic math?

Steve: This one that I begged the counselor to be taken out of at the first of school.[17]

Questions showed that Steve had not experienced

This student is at his job; school rules do not apply here. What if he did not have time after classes to fix his hair for his job? Would it be fair to have a rule that hair has to be kept combed out in school?

any problems with other students because of long hair.
The questioning then moved on to the importance of
long hair for the success of the rock group.

> **Attorney Gibbs:** Why do you feel like it's a necessity?
>
> **Steve:** For the type of music we play. This is something
> that has to go along with our act and it is something
> that a wig cannot cover. If somebody pulled your wig
> off it would be pretty embarrassing and make you look
> pretty bad.[18]

Later on in the questioning, Steve again emphasized
the importance of long hair to the group's music.

> **Steve:** We definitely would not be well accepted with
> short hair.[19]

Another series of questions showed that Steve knew
a number of other boys with long hair who played in
rock groups and who went to schools in the Dallas
Independent School District. It was now time for cross-
examination by the principal's attorneys.

Attorney Franklin Spafford's questioning focused on
the protest song. He established that it was being played
on the radio only two days after school opened and that
it appeared to make fun of Principal Lanham. Steve
insisted that he did not have Principal Lanham in mind
when he wrote it, even when Attorney Spafford asked
about his apology to Principal Lanham.

> **Steve:** The way I made that statement was I asked him

if he had heard the record and if he took any offense to it that I would like to apologize if I did that, I didn't mean to and I also said that we were looking at it from a business standpoint and as far as from an educational standpoint, I told him that we were not knocking him specifically.[20]

The mention of "business standpoint" paved the way for the next series of questions. Did the boys really want an education or did they create the conflict simply to get publicity?

Attorney Spafford: The publicity incident on the refusal to admit you to school because of the hair was helpful in calling attention to the combo, wasn't it? [Rock groups were often called combos in those days.]

Steve: Yes, sir.

Attorney Spafford: And the reason for talking about bringing out the press and television and so forth was to further the entertainment business?

Steve: Yes, sir. I don't believe that the press was there when we tried to get in school. When we got kicked out is when the press arrived.

And further on in the questioning:

Attorney Spafford: I mean it called attention to your combo and led directly to making the record?

Steve: Yes, sir.

Attorney Spafford: That was the subject of the record really?

Steve: Yes, sir.

Attorney Spafford: And Mr. Alexander had the record made, that's his production, isn't it?

Steve: Yes, sir.

Attorney Spafford: That's all.[21]

Now it was Attorney Herbert Hooks's turn. Could he overcome the impression Attorney Spafford had created that the boys were more interested in getting publicity than in getting an education? He asked Steve what he had in mind when he went to school that first day.

> **Steve:** My purpose in going to school on the seventh was to try to get in school and get an understanding that I was a professional musician. I didn't want to be sneaking by Mr. Matthews and Mr. Lanham every time I walked down the hall.
>
> **Attorney Hooks:** Did you arrange for or call any newspapers or radio stations or TV stations to appear upon that day?
>
> **Steve:** No, sir.
>
> **Attorney Hooks:** Did you have any other purpose in mind other than entering school?
>
> **Steve:** No, sir.[22]

Through the rest of the hearing on Thursday and into Friday morning, the boys' attorneys called seven other teenage boys as witnesses. The witnesses, aged fifteen through eighteen, testified that they, too, wore long hair. Most of them played in rock groups and most of them were enrolled in public schools in Texas.

There was also testimony about how common and accepted the longer hairstyle was. One of the witnesses worked after school at a clothes store that featured the new British styles. He personally knew of a number of other longhaired boys at Dallas public schools and testified:

> I believe it is common. It's been around for quite some time and everybody's used to it now. It's no big deal to see a guy walking down the street with hair down about like that and I've seen a few guys with hair past the shoulders which might seem a little uncommon but hair the length of mine or a couple of inches longer is no big deal.[23]

The witnesses were also asked whether or not they had experienced problems because of their long hair. Most of the testimony supported the boys' case, but there were some exceptions. One witness admitted on cross-examination that some of the other boys in school had threatened to cut his hair. The next witness, a senior, admitted that when he was a sophomore he had been involved in a fight with some of the football players over long hair.

But was the trouble really coming from the other students? One of the witnesses was a member of Sounds Unlimited with Paul, Steve, and Phil. He testified that he thought the problem was coming from the school officials:

Most of the comments I've had were last year and they were from fellows who played in sports and it also seemed to me the coaches and the people who were in sports more or less promulgated [promoted] the bad feelings towards the long-haired students of the school and it's not solely our fault, our causing the disturbances—I mean, I've seen the papers written by the coaches denouncing long hair and it seems to me that this promulgates sort of a bad feeling among the students in the school.[24]

This picture of a student with short hair (right) and a student with longer hair (left) illustrates the boys' argument that students with different hairstyles got along together and should be allowed to go to school together, much like black students and white students.

Having presented evidence that the Beatles hairstyle was fairly common and accepted, the boys then called an eighteen-year-old girl to the stand. She testified that she knew football players who wore Mohawks to school. (As she described it, a Mohawk haircut was "shaved off on the sides and hair down the middle."[25]) Surely the Mohawk was more unusual than the Beatles hairstyle, yet the boys with Mohawks were not kept out of school. Then it was Phil's turn to testify.

> **Attorney Hooks:** Have you been ostracized or ignored or abused by fellow students because of your hair?
>
> **Phil:** No, sir, we were all more or less respected and looked up to as musicians.[26]

Phil's cross-examination by Attorney Franklin Spafford went into the making and airing of the protest song. It included the fact that Phil had gone with Mr. Alexander when the song was taken to several Dallas radio stations. Phil denied that the principal referred to in the song was Principal Lanham. He also denied thinking of doing the song until after they had been refused admittance to school. When asked about their request to Principal Lanham on the first day of school, Phil testified:

> Well, we asked to be admitted under the consideration that we were professional musicians and it was necessary to our profession.

> **Attorney Spafford:** In other words, you were asking them to make an exception in your case because of your music work?
>
> **Phil:** Yes, sir.[27]

On redirect, Hooks reemphasized the importance Phil placed on his education:

> **Attorney Hooks:** Do you want to go to school?
>
> **Phil:** Yes, sir, I do.
>
> **Attorney Hooks:** And since the injunction was granted, have you attended Samuell?
>
> **Phil:** Yes, sir, I have.[28]

By the time Phil finished testifying, it was 11 A.M. Friday morning. The court recessed until 2:30 that afternoon. Then, the boys called the owner of a men's clothing shop to the stand.

With the help of the shop owner and several men's fashion magazines, the boys established that the long hairstyle—part of the mod look—was popular and accepted for young men. Further, as the shop owner testified:

> It is shown as a very clean-cut look. The models in there are shown with long hairstyles. They are well-groomed. Their hair has been styled and it's clean and shiny. They are well coordinated with their new hip-hugger pants and wide belts and boots. It is not put forth as a look to be wild or unruly or to cause any sort of commotion. It is a look that is acceptable to a great many people."[29]

Finally, they made the case that the look had its roots in fashions that had all been acceptable for men in the past. The boys had made a case that their hairstyle was not extreme. It was now time to get back to the school rule. The boys called Dr. W. T. White, superintendent of schools for the Dallas Independent School District, to the stand.

Dr. White supported Principal Lanham's decision not to admit the boys to school. They both looked into the school district's *Administrative Policies and Procedures* book. Principal Lanham's action was based on general rules about student attire and conduct. It was also based on Principal Lanham's general responsibility to oversee what happens in school. Then the judge had some questions of his own.

> **Judge Taylor:** All right. Let me ask you a question, Dr. White. You mentioned administrative procedures, have you referred us to the ones that—I mean, in the event of an appeal or anything of that kind from some ruling of the principal, is there some method whereby a student or by and through his parents could appeal to the Superintendent or to the School Board?
>
> **Dr. White:** Your Honor, the first stop would be the Assistant Superintendent of Administration.
>
> **Judge Taylor:** Now, he is mentioned in one of these?
>
> **Dr. White:** Yes. And then, of course, any child or any employee has the right to come to the Superintendent of Schools if he is not satisfied. And then he also has

the legal right to appeal to the Board of Education if it is so desired.

Judge Taylor: And has this particular matter ever been taken by these particular students before the Dallas Board of Education?

Dr. White: No, sir, it hasn't. It has come to the Assistant Superintendent of Administration and through the principal has been related to me.[30]

The judge was asking about the administrative appeal process. Maybe that meant that the judge thought the boys' case was not ripe yet. Maybe they would need to go through the appeal process before a court could consider their case. When the judge asked to see the policy book, Gibbs stepped in.

Gibbs attempted to show that the boys did, in effect, go through every step in the appeal process from principal to assistant superintendent to superintendent to the board, and that at each step, the decision makers had either told the boys—or had told the press—that the principal's decision would be upheld.[31]

The next witness the boys called was their agent, Kent Alexander. It was already clear from prior testimony that Alexander had played a key role in shaping events. He had placed a call to the principal. He had contacted the media, and he had produced the boys' record. It would be helpful to show that Alexander's actions were motivated out of a fatherly concern for the

The principal's authority to regulate hair depended upon whether student hairstyles were "conduct," "attire," (usually clothing) or "speech." Do you think her hairstyle is part of her conduct? Her attire? What she is saying?

boys, rather than a desire for publicity. If that did not work, it would be helpful to show that the desire for publicity was only the agent's, and was not shared by the boys.

So Attorney Herbert Hooks asked the agent why he had called the principal. Because, Mr. Alexander replied, Paul had told him that the dean of girls felt the boys would not be admitted. As a result, Alexander had been concerned both for his business and for the boys.[32]

What about the next day? He was an agent, not a parent; why did he go to the school the next day?

> **Mr. Alexander:** Mr. Jarvis had given me, so to speak, the authority to go to the school and listen to what Mr. Lanham said about Paul's hair and act as a representative for him.[33]
>
> **Attorney Hooks:** Did you make any arrangements with anyone in the news media before you went to school?
>
> **Mr. Alexander:** No.
>
> **Attorney Hooks:** For any publicity whatsoever?
>
> **Mr. Alexander:** No, none at all.[34]

It was after the meeting with the principal that he arranged the publicity.

> **Attorney Hooks:** Do you know whether or not the publicity that ensued was brought about by any of these boys' actions or requests?
>
> **Mr. Alexander:** No, it was not.[35]

On cross-examination, Attorney Spafford questioned just how much fatherly interest Kent Alexander really had.

> **Attorney Spafford:** And the reason you went up to W. W. Samuell on the seventh of September, your idea was to protect your investment?
>
> **Mr. Alexander:** Well, not necessarily that, but as an

agent of my company, of course, but I was also there under the assumption that I was acting as a representative of Paul Jarvis.

Attorney Spafford: Were you there to protect your investment?

Mr. Alexander: I was there to protect my investment.[36]

The next witness was Paul Jarvis. Questions had been raised about the boys' motives. It was important for them to show that they really did want an education.

Attorney Gibbs: Why did you not go directly to your homeroom?

Paul: Because of myself and Mike Holt being there a week previous to enrollment [and] of Mrs. Gilbert saying we would have to talk to Mr. Matthews or Mr. Lanham.

Attorney Gibbs: Now, then, there's been a great deal of testimony about the conference on the seventh and why you boys did not go into school. Upon this date were you given the opportunity to attend classes?

Paul: Yes, sir, I was.

Attorney Gibbs: I'll ask you whether or not there was any qualifications upon you attending classes, you individually, Paul?

Paul: Yes, sir, there was.

Attorney Gibbs: What was the qualification?

Paul: Mr. Lanham stated that I could enroll today but tomorrow I would have to appear with my hair trimmed up because of it being a necessity or something of that sort.[37]

So Paul was required to trim his hair to go to school, just like Phil and Steve.

Paul's attorney then led him though a series of questions that brought out the boys' efforts to get into school. They had gone to the general administration building Wednesday afternoon, but were told by the assistant superintendent that the superintendent was not available to meet with them. They had gone back to school again on Thursday but were refused. They then went to seven different schools to try to get admitted, but without success. After all that, they still went back to W. W. Samuell the following Tuesday to try to get in.

On cross-examination, Paul confirmed that when Kent Alexander had come to the school "he was acting as my father that day as my father had instructed him."[38] And he denied that Alexander had said, "Remember what I told you to say." Paul had heard Alexander say, "You boys keep a cool head and be respectable."[39]

Attorney Spafford also asked Paul about the protest song.

> **Attorney Spafford:** Did the publicity involved here have anything to do with your thinking about this song?
>
> **Paul:** No, sir, it was just on the basis of us not being admitted to school. We kind of—well, I guess you feel

odd sometimes and you want to tell your troubles and I guess this is a good way of doing it.[40]

Paul also denied that the song was intended to make fun of Principal Lanham.

> **Attorney Spafford:** You didn't mention his name, but I mean he's the only principal that you dealt with?
>
> **Paul:** He wasn't the only principal we talked to, no, sir, we talked to quite a few.[41]

After Paul's cross-examination was completed, the boys' presentation of their case ended.

5

The Case for the Principal

As soon as the boys had finished presenting their case, one of the principal's attorneys wanted the judge to declare victory for the school. The judge refused. The school's attorney, Mr. Whitham, tried again, arguing strongly that:

> There's been no evidence that there has been any abuse of any authority or any discretion in the government of this high school, we ask the temporary injunction be denied and the temporary restraining order be set aside and the conduct of the high school returned to the lawful authorities.[1]

It was not enough to persuade the judge. Again he overruled the school's motion to dismiss. He then firmly asked Attorney Whitham whether the school intended to close its case without presenting any evidence.

Losing the argument must have surprised the attorney, because he replied that the school had not decided whether to offer evidence. But the judge twice overruled the school's request to dismiss the lawsuit, so maybe the judge thought the boys had made a case. Attorney Whitham asked for a few moments to think.

The school called Lee A. McShan, Jr., president of the board of education for the Dallas Independent School District, to the stand.

> **Attorney Spafford:** What I'm asking you is, do you approve or disapprove of the action of Mr. Lanham in this instance case?
>
> **Mr. McShan:** I certainly approve of the action of Mr. Lanham. In this case he is charged with the normal and ordinary operation of a Dallas high school.[2]

On cross-examination, the boys' attorney asked questions to show that the president's approval was publicly announced before the boys filed their lawsuit. Since the board of education was the final step in the administrative appeal process, this would help the boys make their argument that their case was ripe for consideration by the court.

The judge himself, however, finished the questioning on whether the board of education had taken any official action. The board president had made a public statement. Even if the board members had discussed it among themselves and agreed that the principal was right, it would not necessarily have persuaded the judge. As Judge Taylor said, "I wouldn't attempt to think of any conversation between members of the Board as an official action of the Board."[3]

After Mr. McShan's cross-examination was completed, the judge concluded that it would be impossible to finish that Friday. He declared a recess until the following Monday morning.[4]

At 10 A.M. Monday morning, September 26, the school's attorneys called the boys' agent to the stand. Through his questions, Attorney Spafford established that the media had arrived at the school approximately thirty minutes after the first meeting with the principal ended, and that Mr. Alexander had called quite a few to come.

The school's attorney then turned to the making of the protest record. Over objection from the boys' attorney, he played the record for the judge. This way the judge could make up his own mind about it. It was an experience Judge Taylor would later describe as "an excursion into cacophony."[5] (The judge thought it sounded more like noise than like music.)

Attorney Spafford then started to explore the agent's responsibility to get publicity for his rock groups. The exchange between the lawyer and the agent got pretty heated:

> **Judge:** One at a time now. Let him finish, Mr. Spafford, or don't you start Mr. Alexander until he gets through asking. Talk one at a time and not together.[6]

Eventually it led to the point that Attorney Spafford wanted to make.

> **Attorney Spafford:** Is it not a major part of your job to publicize and get known your folks that you book?
>
> **Mr. Alexander:** Right. If you want to look at it from the point of view of newspapers and records and different advertising media, yes.

And a little further on in the questioning:

> **Attorney Spafford:** And that's what you were doing when you called the *News,* the *Herald* and KBOX, KLIF, WFAA, KRLD and WBAP to come to W. W. Samuell on September the 7th, didn't you?
>
> **Mr. Alexander:** One could say that, yes.
>
> **Attorney Spafford:** Yes, and haven't you followed through and taken advantage of every opportunity to publicize this incident since?
>
> **Mr. Alexander:** I certainly have.[7]

Spafford had made his point. Mr. Alexander had a strong business interest in the boys. Any publicity over the boys' hairstyles at school might generate record sales and bookings.

Now it was Attorney Herbert Hooks's turn to cross-examine the witness. He needed to show that the publicity-seeking came afterward, that it was not part of the boys' efforts to get into school. As he did that, he drew from Mr. Alexander a statement that reflects how many people feel about change.

> **Attorney Hooks:** Why did you do it, Mr. Alexander?
>
> **Mr. Alexander:** In the first place, how can anyone ever settle outdated and outmoded rules without raising a controversy over them?
>
> **Attorney Hooks:** Did you talk to the three boys about the fact that you were going to call the news media before you did?
>
> **Mr. Alexander:** I didn't.

Later on in the questioning:

> **Attorney Hooks:** Had you discussed any possible publicity before the day you went to school?
>
> **Mr. Alexander:** No, sir, I hadn't.
>
> **Attorney Hooks:** Was there any plan by you or in conjunction with the three boys to cause an incident at school which would result in publicity?
>
> **Mr. Alexander:** None.[8]

There was just one final point that Attorney Spafford wanted to make on redirect examination before Mr. Alexander left the stand:

> **Attorney Spafford:** I'm asking you if you have a commercial interest in this whole transaction in dollars and cents?

Mr. Alexander: I certainly do.

Attorney Spafford: Thank you. That's all.[9]

The school's lawyers then called Principal Lanham back to the stand. Through careful questioning, they established the fact that the trouble with longhaired boys started two to three years ago. It had started with about three or four boys the first year, then eight or nine, then last year about eight or nine boys again. This year, the year they had just started, the principal was not aware of over ten or twelve boys with long hair if that many.[10]

But out of how many students? If there were only ten or twelve boys in the school, that would be everybody. How many students were there at W. W. Samuell High School?

> **Principal Lanham:** Approximately twenty-four hundred.
>
> **Attorney Spafford:** Twenty-four hundred, and how many boys are in W. W. Samuell today?
>
> **Principal Lanham:** They outnumber the girls by a few. There are over 1,200 boys and less than 1,200 girls.[11]

Having established that long hair was relatively rare in the school, the attorney turned to the boys' claim that they were discriminated against.

> **Attorney Spafford:** Now, Mr. Lanham, in dealing with the three Plaintiffs that are involved in this suit, have

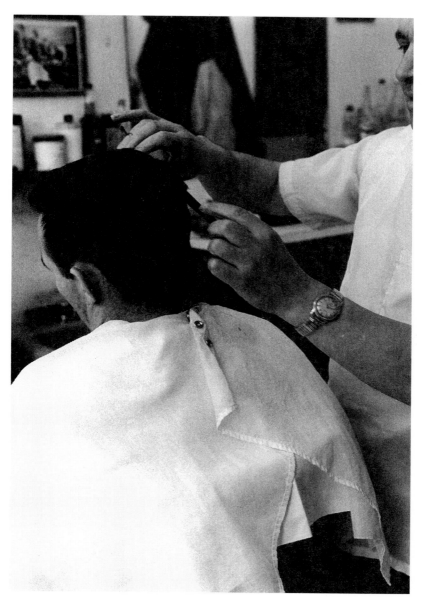

This 1968 picture gives you a closer look at the short hairstyle that the principal testified was more common.

you dealt with those three boys any differently than the other students in your school?

Principal Lanham: No.

Attorney Spafford: Have you treated these three boys exactly as you have treated the others?

Principal Lanham: Yes.

Attorney Spafford: Have you treated these three boys unfairly in any way?

Principal Lanham: I don't think so. I certainly have attempted not to.[12]

On cross-examination, Attorney Hooks explored with the principal whether the boys' protest song was really that offensive. If Principal Lanham did not find it offensive, then it would be harder to think of the song as evidence that the boys had a bad attitude about school. On the other hand, if the principal *did* find it offensive, that might suggest that he made his decision based on spite.

Attorney Hooks: Your close friends don't take it very seriously do they, Mr. Lanham?

Principal Lanham: Yes, they do. Some of them are highly incensed about it.

Attorney Hooks: Are you personally offended by the record itself?

Principal Lanham: Well, I might answer that in this way, I don't appreciate that, just like the boys said, they were not proud of it when I talked to them the other day and I don't think you would appreciate it very much if you were held up for ridicule.[13]

The questioning continued.

> **Attorney Hooks:** You do take the record as directed towards you personally rather than just a general protest song about hair?
>
> **Principal Lanham:** Well, I can very well—you can't very well consider it any other way since the events happened as they did.[14]

Remember, the boys had testified that there were no problems during the time that they had been in school under court order; even the principal had testified to that. Why not let the boys go to school with their hair the way it was and require a haircut only if problems really did develop?

> **Attorney Hooks:** Mr. Lanham, don't you think it would have been a wiser course to follow to do as you've done in every instance in the past with boys with long hair, that is to allow them to go to school and then if a disciplinary problem arose, then take such action as might be required under the circumstances?
>
> **Principal Lanham:** No.
>
> **Attorney Hooks:** Don't you feel that would have been a wiser course of action rather than excluding these three boys from enrolling at all?
>
> **Principal Lanham:** No, they weren't completely excluded. They were asked to trim their hair and they said they were not going to trim their hair that they were going to let it grow.[15]

Questioning continued.

Attorney Hooks: Ordinarily, you wouldn't try to anticipate problems or the handling of them as an administrator. . . .

Principal Lanham: (interrupting) I wouldn't try to anticipate problems in the handling of a school? That's about as far afield as you can get if you don't anticipate the handling of the school situation and trying to keep it where those things don't occur.[16]

Finally, questioning came to the following point:

Attorney Hooks: You consider this a serious enough problem to anticipate any difficulties you may have?

Principal Lanham: It has been in the past.

Attorney Hooks: But it has never been serious enough to exclude people from a public education?

Principal Lanham: It has been serious enough that we have on record the suspension of a boy until he did trim his hair.[17]

But surely not all longhaired boys were problems. Attorney Hooks tried to nail down with his questions that no complaints had been made against Paul, Phil, and Steve. But when he pushed on that point, Principal Lanham testified that Phil received twenty-nine detentions the year before, for being "tardy, cutting school the last two periods, truancy one day and misconduct out of class."[18]

Maybe, as in Steve's case, the problems were caused by his work outside of school, not by his hair.

> **Attorney Hooks:** Do you know how many hours a
> week he was working?
>
> **Principal Lanham:** No, when we know about these
> things we try to counsel with the parents and explain
> to them that they shouldn't be working so much that
> it will interfere with their school work.[19]

Responding to that would have to wait until the
boys could bring on other witnesses. But there was
another thing that the boys' attorneys wanted to get
across while Principal Lanham was still on the stand. On
re-cross-examination, Attorney Hooks tried to bring out
the fact that the boys really did want to go to school.

> **Attorney Hooks:** You have a doubt in your mind that
> they came up there to enroll in school and wanted an
> education?
>
> **Principal Lanham:** They were ready to enroll in
> school on their terms that they would be allowed to
> wear their hair long and let it continue to grow. And
> that way I think they would have enrolled, yes, if I
> would have let them enroll under those circumstances.
>
> **Attorney Hooks:** Well, you were pretty disgusted with
> them and their parents and the many times that they
> came up there to see you and surely you're of the opin-
> ion that they did want to go to school?
>
> **Principal Lanham:** Yes, under their conditions.[20]

And with that, Attorney Hooks ended his questioning and the school's lawyers ended their presentation of
evidence.

The boys did not want to end with the testimony

Does this 1970 picture illustrate Principal Lanham's argument that longer-haired students did not respect rules and caused trouble? Would making the students in the picture cut their hair also make them stop doing this?

about Phil's detentions and how rare long hair was in school. Since the school had finished its turn, the boys now had an opportunity to call some witnesses of their own.

When the court came back into session, the boys' attorneys called a student at the school to the stand. He named shorthaired boys he knew who had graduated from W. W. Samuell "with considerably more than 29 detentions."[21] He also testified that he knew all three of the boys and that he had not observed any trouble surrounding them because of their hair.

Next the boys called a sixteen-year-old boy to the stand who not only went to school at W. W. Samuell, but also worked part-time as a barber. Under questioning by Attorney Hooks, he reported that "a considerable amount of people are wearing their hair like that" and that he had not seen any disruption in the classrooms or halls because of it.[22] He also offered an opinion that, as it turned out, was to be echoed much later in a much higher court: "I think that every individual has a right to wear his hair to his own taste."[23]

Finally, the boys called Kent Alexander back to the stand. Herbert Hooks reconfirmed how common and accepted longer hair was for male entertainers in television programs, movies, and rock groups.

Both sides then declared that they were finished presenting evidence. The court recessed until 2:00 P.M., when the attorneys for both sides were to present closing arguments.

Unfortunately, the attorneys' final arguments were not recorded in the hearing transcript. But after they had finished, Judge Taylor addressed both sides:

> I'll say this, the Court has not taken this matter lightly. And I hope that the courts never do get to the point where they don't have time enough or interest enough in matters this important to where they treat them

lightly and I hope I don't disappoint anyone, but I want to deliberate myself on this matter. I will take the matter under advisement, rendering no decision or determination today, but I will call you back and you may expect to hear from me very shortly.[24]

Herbert Hooks asked the judge if he would consider allowing the boys to continue their studies in the meantime. The judge refused, promising that "my decision will be forthcoming within a matter of a couple of days."[25]

6

What Happened in Federal District Court?

True to his word, Judge Taylor wrote a letter to the attorneys on both sides that Friday, September 30, 1966, to let them know what his decision was. It was short and to the point.

> Gentlemen:
>
> Upon consideration of the evidence in [this] case, I have concluded that the Application for Temporary Injunction should be denied.
>
> Among other reasons for this decision, it does not appear that Mr. Lanham, the Principal, nor Dr. White, the Superintendent, acted arbitrarily, capriciously, nor unreasonably in refusing to admit the minor plaintiffs to the classrooms of W. W. Samuell High School. The conditions or terms upon which a public free education are granted in the high schools of Texas cannot be fixed nor determined by the pupils

themselves. Nor is a contract which is unenforceable against the minor plaintiffs in this State to be considered as determinative of the right.

Let an appropriate order be prepared by the attorneys.

Written opinion will follow.

Yours very truly,
W. M. Taylor, Jr.
United States District Judge[1]

Judge Taylor was saying that he would not order the principal to admit the boys with their long hair. The adults running the school were the best ones to decide how a public education should be provided—not the students. Principal Lanham had not acted unreasonably when he required the boys to get their hair trimmed. The judge also did not believe that the boys' contract with their agent needed to be considered. Since the contract could not force the boys to have long hair (because they were not adults), the contract would not be enough to force the principal to allow the boys to attend school.

While this short letter made it clear that the boys lost their main argument, the longer written opinion (which came out on December 9, 1966) made it clear that the boys *had* won some very important secondary points.

For example, the first issue had been whether the

court had jurisdiction to hear the case at all. The opinion discussed whether the boys' case was ripe enough for the court to hear or whether the boys should have gone through the administrative appeal process first. The judge decided that under the federal law the boys had used (the Civil Rights Act), students did not have to finish the public school appeal process before going to federal court.

Next, the judge turned to the school's argument that the boys' case should not be heard by a federal court because their concerns were frivolous and insubstantial. But the judge agreed with the boys. Quoting from *Brown* v. *Board of Education* and from the Texas constitution, he made the point that getting a public education was very important, indeed.[2] So the boys won their arguments about the federal court's ability to decide their case.

After explaining in his opinion why his court could rule on the boys' concerns, the judge then proceeded to do exactly that. He wrote that the boys' case had "received a great deal of publicity and had aroused a great deal of feeling in the community. It is felt therefore that we should say more than merely whether or not this Court has jurisdiction to rule on this case."[3]

The judge used the following principles to guide him to his conclusion:

1) "Since confusion and anarchy have no place in the classroom, school authorities must control the behavior of their students."[4]

2) "It is inconceivable that a school administrator could operate his school successfully if required by the courts to follow the dictates of the students as to what their appearance shall be, what they shall wear, what hours they will attend, etc."[5]

3) However, school authority must be exercised with restraint and reasonableness, particularly "where the effects of the regulation extend beyond the classroom and bear directly on the student's person and his freedom of expression" and where it would "impinge on the student's freedom and the individual parent's right to raise his child as he sees fit."[6]

When he balanced the needs of the boys against the needs of the school, the judge leaned in the direction of the school. "This court is concerned for the welfare of the individual plaintiffs in this case, but feels that the rights of other students, and the interest of teachers, administrators and the community at large are paramount."[7]

So the judge did not think that the school authorities did anything wrong. "On the contrary, it appears that they acted reasonably under the circumstances, taking into consideration these individual students *and* [emphasis added] the need for an academic atmosphere."[8]

In coming to his conclusion, the judge was also influenced by the evidence suggesting that the whole thing might have been planned by the boys' agent just to get publicity. The judge thought that the telephone call to the principal's home the night before, the confrontation in the principal's office the next day, the immediate release of a protest song, and the news interviews were all very suspicious.[9]

While the judge had heard the boys' arguments that, despite their agent, the boys themselves still wanted an education, he thought that "they want this education on their own terms."[10] The judge concluded, "The terms upon which a public free education is granted in the high schools of Texas cannot be fixed or determined by the pupils themselves."[11]

What about the contract? Did it make any difference that the boys were under a contract with the agent to keep their hair in the Beatles hairstyle? No. Because they were not adults when they signed it (in legal terms, they were "minors"), the agent could not have sued them in court to make them do what the contract said; in the language lawyers use, the contract was "unenforceable." So the judge dismissed the contract argument the same way he had dismissed it in his letter, with one sentence: "Nor is a contract which is unenforceable against the minor plaintiffs in this State to be considered determinative of the right."[12]

So where did this leave the boys? They had convinced the judge that federal courts should hear student concerns about things like this. They had also convinced the judge that students did not have to complete the school appeal process before going to federal court. But the judge decided that they had to get their hair trimmed before they could go to school. What would they do now?

7

What Happened in Federal Appeals Court?

The boys decided to take their case to the court at the next highest level—the federal appeals court. The appeals court is not supposed to hear a case all over again. It is only supposed to check if the trial court handled the case correctly. This is not the place to bring up new legal grounds and new legal arguments. Instead, the boys had to argue that the trial court had made a legal mistake in the way it had handled the case.

The original lawyers representing the boys, Herbert Hooks and Dan Gibbs, were joined in their appeal by Marvin Menaker and W. D. Masterson.

The American Civil Liberties Union (ACLU) also provided some assistance to the boys at this stage. The

ACLU is a private organization that was created in order to help protect the rights and liberties given to people under the United States Constitution. The ACLU has assisted in many landmark cases about individual rights.[1]

In their appeal, the boys argued that Judge Taylor's decision was "an abuse of discretion." They argued that his decision was not consistent with the law. They argued that it was clear that the action of the school authorities was against the law under the constitution and the laws of Texas.

Further, they argued that the length and style of their hair was a form of expression—just like thought and speech are forms of expression—and that freedom of expression was protected by the United States Constitution. So requiring the boys to change their hairstyle before they could attend school was unconstitutional.

The boys had originally based their case on the Civil Rights Act and they could not make new legal arguments at this level. So how could the boys make a freedom of expression argument now? Judge Taylor had mentioned it in his opinion. The boys might have argued that, since Judge Taylor clearly had it in mind when he made his decision, it was an argument before the court, and that is why they could argue it on appeal.

If freedom of expression is protected, the boys' argument continued, then they should receive double protection. Their hairstyle was more than a whim, it was a necessity. They were required by their contract to keep their hair that way. Even if it were not required by contract, their hairstyle was necessary if they were to succeed in their chosen career. The boys also repeated their trial court argument that the school's action was discriminatory and, therefore, illegal under the federal Civil Rights Act.

The boys also felt that in view of the fact that they had a reasonable chance of winning their case, Judge Taylor should have ordered them admitted to school during court arguments. Since Judge Taylor did not do that, his decision was an abuse of discretion and should be overturned.

Meanwhile, the principal and the school district saw it differently. Their lawyers argued that there were at least two other cases that ruled that a school could keep students out until they had received an acceptable haircut. Further, the contract should not count because the boys were minors. So, their lawyers argued, the judge did not make a mistake; he had plenty of room under the law to decide the way he did.

On December 12, 1966, the full 330-page transcript of the boys' hearing and all the exhibits were sent to the appeals court. The boys had submitted fifty-one exhibits during the hearing, including photographs of the boys themselves and of other rock groups; the school district had submitted three exhibits. Both sides argued that all this evidence proved that their side was right. Then they waited over a year to see what the appeals court would decide.

The Appellate Court Decision

The boys' case was ruled on by three judges of the United States Court of Appeals for the Fifth Circuit.

The boys argued that their hairstyle was a necessity. These Hopi girls are wearing a hairstyle dictated by their culture. Would it be right for a school to say they could not wear their hair like this?

One wrote the court opinion, the second agreed with him, and the third wrote a dissenting opinion that disagreed with the other two. It was a close call, but which way did it go?

Issued on March 29, 1968, the majority opinion started by disagreeing that Principal Lanham's action was against Texas law. (The majority opinion is the one that more than half of the judges agree with.) The court noted the problems that had been caused in the boys' school over long hair. It concluded that Principal Lanham's actions were reasonable and within the scope of discretion granted to him by the Texas constitution and laws.

Next, the majority opinion turned to freedom of expression. Interestingly enough, the judges did not weigh the pros and cons of whether a hairstyle was a form of expression. They assumed that it was, and started from there. In the language of the court, "We shall assume, though we do not decide, for the purposes of this opinion that a hairstyle is a constitutionally protected mode of expression."[2]

But if the right to choose your own hairstyle is protected by the United States Constitution, doesn't that decide the case right there? Doesn't that mean that the principal could not tell the boys to get a haircut?

No. The rule that guided the court was that the state

(in this case, the school system set up and funded by the state) could cut back on the boys' freedom of expression if—and only if—the school had a justifiable reason. In lawyer's language, the school had to have a "compelling" reason. Did Principal Lanham have a compelling reason? The majority opinion thought he did. The judge who wrote the opinion thought that the compelling reason was the state's need to maintain an effective and efficient school system.

To show how the balance between individual rights and state's rights works, the court discussed two cases about schools that would not let students wear freedom buttons. (Freedom buttons were buttons showing support for civil rights.) The two cases had been decided by this same appeals court on the same day. In one case, the school won. In the other case, the students won.

What was the difference? In the case that upheld the school rule, the evidence presented at trial clearly demonstrated that wearing freedom buttons interfered with the operation of the school. In the case the students won, there was no evidence that the buttons interfered.

The majority opinion then went on to discuss several other cases about students who were not admitted to school until they got an acceptable haircut. Two of those cases held that the haircut regulation was acceptable. The rule was reasonably necessary to maintain school discipline.

The majority opinion pointed out another hairstyle case, though, in which the court had ruled in favor of the students. In that case, the evidence showed that the school administrators banned certain hairstyles only because they did not like them.

There was no evidence that the haircuts had any effect on the health, discipline, or decorum of the school. Those administrators lost. Principal Lanham, however, had never expressed a personal dislike for the boys' long hair.

The majority opinion also recognized that the boys were professional musicians. They had a constitutionally protected right to follow their chosen occupation free from unreasonable governmental interference. But the majority opinion concluded that Principal Lanham's action *was* reasonable because the boys could wear wigs. The majority opinion also noted that at this time in the boys' lives, school might be more important to them than their after-school jobs. Returning to the civil rights argument, the argument that had been central to the boys' case in the trial court, the majority opinion dismissed it in only nine words: "we find no violation of the civil rights statutes."[3]

Consequently the court concluded that there was no

This American Indian girl has chosen braids for her hairstyle.

abuse of discretion. Judge Taylor had conducted a full
hearing giving each side an opportunity to present witnesses and submit documents. Then he had come to a
reasoned opinion. The appeals court supported that
decision.

The dissenting opinion, written by Judge Tuttle, was
short but strongly in favor of the boys. Judge Tuttle was
deeply concerned that three students were "denied a
high school education because the length of their hair
did not suit the school authorities."[4]

Judge Tuttle agreed that their hairstyle was a constitutionally protected form of expression and did not
think the principal's reason was compelling. Further,
the judge said:

> It appears to me, without the slightest doubt, that this
> is an utterly unreasonable classification of students by
> the state in granting or denying the right of a public
> education. This, of course, if true, is violative of the
> 14th Amendment.[5]

The judge was saying that it was not logical to
divide students into groups based on their hair length,
and to provide a public education only to shorthaired
students. That would be illegal under the Fourteenth
Amendment to the United States Constitution.

Judge Tuttle recognized that the principal's case was
based on concern that other students might cause

91

trouble. He pointed out that a person's freedom of speech should not be denied simply because someone might disagree with that person.

Finally, Judge Tuttle brought up a point that had not been raised before. Freedom to choose one's own hairstyle is protected by the United States Constitution; beating up other students is not. If the school is going to prohibit anything, it should prohibit the violence it feels could possibly result, and not the hairstyle itself.

What Do the Boys Do Now?

The strong dissent must have been encouraging, particularly since only one judge would have had to change his mind for the boys to win. The boys requested a rehearing of their case. The rehearing was denied on April 30, 1968.

Now what? Should they take their case to the United States Supreme Court? Remember, by this time their senior year had come and gone, and the following school year was almost over, too. Going to the Supreme Court could take a while and cost even more money than they had spent already. Would they do it?

8

What Happened at the Supreme Court?

The boys did decide to appeal to the Supreme Court. They filed a petition for a writ of *certiorari* (a request for the Supreme Court to consider their case) on June 1, 1968.

Thousands of cases are appealed to the Supreme Court every year. It is impossible for the Supreme Court to consider them all. It only hears the most important ones. With so many to choose from, the Justices can have very different opinions about which cases are the most important. If four Supreme Court Justices think they should hear a case, the case is accepted for argument and decision. Today the Court hears only about 2 percent of the approximately seven thousand petitions filed each year.

The boys' lawyers, Menaker, Gibbs, Hooks, and Masterson, argued in their petition to the Supreme Court that the boys' case presented "important issues of interference with constitutional rights of free expression as the basis of denying [the boys] a free public school education."[1] Picking up on Appellate Judge Tuttle's point that violence and not hairstyle should be prohibited, their petition argued that instead of protecting the boys' rights to freedom of expression, the lower court opinions in the boys' case had the effect of protecting the troublemakers' "rights" to harass students with long hair.

The majority opinion seemed to require more conformity of the boys than the law says should be required in a free society. The boys' lawyers strengthened their argument with the following quote from the Supreme Court's *West Virginia Board of Education* v. *Barnette* decision:

> If there is any fixed star in our constitutional constellation, it is that no official high or petty, can prescribe what shall be orthodox in politics, nationalism, religion, or other matters of opinion or force citizens to confess by word or act their faith therein. If there are any circumstances which permit an exception, they do not now occur to us.[2]

They argued that the lower court decisions in the boys' case were completely out of line with Texas law on students' rights to a free public education. They cited three cases in which Texas state courts had ruled that a Texas school's authority to deny enrollment or to suspend students was limited.

Finally, they argued, the way the federal courts had dismissed the boys' civil rights argument made it seem as though the Civil Rights Act only applied to racial discrimination. But the act says that states and other governmental bodies cannot deprive *any* citizen of his

This group picture of the United States Supreme Court Justices was taken around 1968.

95

or her rights. The Supreme Court should take the boys' case, they said, so it could make the important point that the Civil Rights Act was not limited to race.

The lawyers for Principal Lanham and the Dallas Independent School District also submitted written arguments to the Supreme Court. They were trying to convince the Supreme Court *not* to hear the case. Principal Lanham's decision had been upheld by the district court and the court of appeals; if the Supreme

Should school rules about student appearance also cover face painting? Is face painting all right for school? Is makeup all right for school? When does it stop being makeup and start being face painting?

Court did not hear the case, Principal Lanham could still require the boys to get a haircut. Their brief in opposition was filed on June 27, 1968.

A brief is the document lawyers give to the court explaining why their clients should win. After giving a summary of the facts that were most helpful to their view of the case, the lawyers for the school argued that hairstyle was not really speech. It did not communicate any idea. They pointed out that these three boys did not explain what their hair was trying to say. They also argued that whatever rights the boys had in their hairstyle were only limited enough to permit a reasonable learning environment for everyone in the school. That did not violate the United States Constitution.

They also argued that the principal's action was not unlawful under Texas law. They distinguished the three cases quoted by the boys' lawyers by noting that two involved student marriage and one involved a student who became a mother. They then went on to cite other cases that, they argued, showed that the principal did have the right under Texas law to do what he did.

Finally, they argued that there had been no violation of the Civil Rights Act. They argued that the civil rights laws should not be applied to situations that did not involve racial discrimination. It was the end of June;

both sides had submitted briefs to the Supreme Court. It was now up to the Supreme Court to decide what would happen next.

The Court's Action

On October 14, 1968, the Supreme Court announced that it would *not* hear the boys' case. As is usual, it did not have to explain why. But at least one of the Justices disagreed. Justice Douglas thought the Court should hear the case. He wrote two powerful paragraphs explaining why he thought so.

What he said was that from the very beginning of the United States, starting with the Declaration of Independence, there was the fundamental concept that each person should be free to be himself or herself. As the country was established, this concept was written into the very document that formed it and gave it shape—the United States Constitution. Surely, if the Constitution stood for anything, it stood for the freedom of each person to choose what he or she looks like.

Local governments provide many services to the people who live within their boundaries. It would be ridiculous to prevent the fire department from going to someone's house if it was on fire, or to stop the police from answering a call for help, or to stop picking up

Justice William O. Douglas tried to convince other Supreme Court Justices to hear the boys' case.

someone's trash simply because that person chose to look different. Not giving someone a public education for that reason should be just as unacceptable.

Justice Douglas could not persuade enough of the other Supreme Court Justices to agree with him, and the boys' case ended there.

9

What Happened Next?

Phil, Steve, and Paul had wanted to finished their education at W. W. Samuell High School *and* have successful careers as rock musicians.[1] It appears as if they got neither, at least not in the obvious way.

First, Dallas Independent School District records show only that a Steve Webb graduated on May 23, 1970, about a year and a half after the Supreme Court action.[2] (This timing would suggest that Steve had started —and finished—the first full school year after the Supreme Court had decided not to hear the case.) There is no indication in the administrative records that a Dallas Independent School District diploma was issued to Phillip Ferrell or Paul Jarvis.[3]

Now, this does not mean that the boys never got an education. They may have finished their high school education somewhere else. What it does suggest is that, except perhaps for Steve, the boys did not finish their education in the public school system they had sued.

But what about their music careers? Did they become famous rock musicians? It does not look like it. There is no entry for Paul Jarvis, Steve Webb, Phil Ferrell, or their rock group, Sounds Unlimited, in *The Harmony Illustrated Encyclopedia of Rock*. Nor are they mentioned in either the index or "The Sound of Texas" chapter in *The Rolling Stones Illustrated History of Rock & Roll*.

This does not mean that they were not able to make a living as musicians. They may have. They may even have become famous under other names; we do not know. What it does suggest is that they did not achieve musical success to the extent that they must have hoped at the time they filed their lawsuit.

This is not unusual; lawsuits do not always get people what they are hoping for when they file them. Does this mean that the lawsuit was a waste? Not at all. It did have an impact on the way students were treated by their public schools.

Remember, we learned in Chapter 6 that the boys won their argument that their concerns should be heard in court. A guide for public school principals was written after the boys had won. It warned principals that courts would accept lawsuits about suspending or expelling students because of their hairstyle. The guide explained that for the public school to win, the school and the principal would have to show that keeping the unusually styled students out of school was necessary— either to protect the students from harm or to protect the educational process from being disrupted. In other words, the guide warned principals that they could not keep a student out of school simply because they did not like the student's hairstyle.[4]

Even though the Supreme Court had decided not to hear the boys' case, other organizations were listening. The American Federation of Teachers voted in 1970 to support student "freedom of speech and expression, including a choice of one's own dress and grooming."[5]

The boys' case was also mentioned in a very important law journal. A note published in 1971 in the *Harvard Law Review* referred to the boys' case several times. It argued that "no high school [should] be able to expel a long-haired student until it has succeeded in showing that it has a real and compelling need to do so."[6]

In addition to published articles and school policy, Phil, Paul, and Steve's lawsuit also had an influence in the courts. It was among the first of a wave of lawsuits over the extent to which schools could regulate students' hairstyles. In January 1972, Justice Douglas noted in his dissent to *Olff* v. *East Side Union High School District* that "There are well over 50 reported cases squarely presenting the issue, students having won in about half of them."[7] In March 1972, Justice Douglas noted in his dissent to *Freeman, Guardian, et al.* v. *Flake et al.* that eight of the twelve federal circuits had ruled on the question of whether a student could be kept out of school because of his hairstyle; four upheld the school hair regulations and four struck them down.[8] In both of these dissents, Justice Douglas specifically referred to Phil, Paul, and Steve's lawsuit as he urged the other Justices to hear a student hairstyle case.

The boys' case was also mentioned by name in one of the most important cases dealing with the constitutional rights of students in public schools.[9] In *Tinker* v. *Des Moines* in 1969, the Supreme Court stated that, "Students in school as well as out of school are 'persons' under our Constitution. They are possessed of fundamental rights which the State must respect. . . ."[10]

The *Tinker* court focused on students' freedom of speech, noting that "Freedom of expression would not truly exist if the right could be exercised only in an area that [the school] has provided as a safe [place] for crackpots."[11] Therefore, the majority opinion explained, students are not limited to expressing their

Longer hair eventually did become much more common and accepted among students. This photograph of medical students was taken in 1972. Compare their hair length with the 1966 student picture on page 12.

views only at the times and places established for classroom discussion, but:

> when [the student] is in the cafeteria, or on the playing field, or on the campus during the authorized hours, he may express his opinions, even on controversial subjects . . . if he does so without materially and substantially interfering with the requirements of appropriate discipline in the operation of the school and without colliding with the rights of others. But conduct by the student, in class or out of it, which for any reason—whether it stems from time, place, or type of behavior—materially disrupts classwork or involves substantial disorder or invasion of the rights

of others [can be stopped and disciplined by the school authority].[12]

The Supreme Court said that students have rights when in schools. Students cannot exercise those rights in a way that would hurt others, however. Students must exercise their rights responsibly. The full sentence at the end of the first *Tinker* quote read, "They are possessed of fundamental rights which the State must respect, just as they themselves must respect their obligations to the State."[13]

10

Where Does This Issue Stand Today?

You might think that the issue of student hairstyles in public school was settled long ago. After all, many of today's parents were the same people who fought for and wore long hair when they were teenagers. However, this issue is still with us today, and this time it is even more complicated than it was before.

Here are some of the things that have happened more recently:

- High school students in Mandeville, Louisiana, picketed to protest school board rules limiting how long boys' hair could be.[1]

- About sixty boys in Henry County, Georgia, were sent home from school for violating a school rule that their hair could not be long enough to touch the bottoms of their collars.[2]

- Most of Port Sulphur, Louisiana's, graduating high school class planned to stay away from its graduation ceremony in protest. Protest what? The school superintendent had said that an honors student could not attend the graduation ceremony because his hair was too long. But a few days later, the honor student trimmed his hair and was permitted to go to the ceremony.[3]

- Because of disputes over student hair length in several Texas schools, a committee in the Texas state House of Representatives planned to propose a law that would limit the punishment a school could impose on longhaired students.[4] (This is another way to deal with a conflict. Instead of going to court, try to get a law passed.)

- The Spring Independent School District in Texas had a rule that boys could not wear their hair below their collar (or below the collar seam in their T-shirt, if they were not wearing a shirt with a collar). So a couple of ponytailed boys came to school in wigs; that way they could have short hair at school but long hair everywhere else. Then the school district changed their rules to ban wigs, too.[5]

- There was an eight-year-old student in Texas who was put in a ten-foot by thirteen-foot isolation room by his school every school day for four months because he wore a seven-inch ponytail.[6] (Ten feet by thirteen feet is smaller than a typical school room, but would be a reasonable bedroom.)

- In 1995, the Texas Supreme Court (a state court) upheld a public school rule against long hair and earrings for boys. This was a particularly interesting case because the high school student who sued was not a child; he was old enough to be considered an adult under Texas law.

- The argument can go the other way, too. A private church school in California told a valedictorian student that he could not come to his eighth-grade graduation because his hair was too short.[7]

- A public school in Illinois had a policy that did not allow boys to wear hairstyles such as corn rows, dreadlocks, and braids. The school changed the policy after parents and students argued that the policy was unfair to African-American students. The school had originally adopted the hairstyle policy because it felt that the forbidden styles signaled gang membership.[8]

- Two girls in a junior high school in Chicago were pulled from class because they came to school with zigzag parts in their hair. The school policy against wearing what the school considered "symbols" in student hairstyles was intended to cut down on gang influence in the school.[9]

Incidentally, as we saw in Chapter 2, it is not just in the United States that people argue about what student heads should look like. Egyptian students have clashed with Egyptian school authorities over whether girls could wear traditional head coverings worn by Muslims that partially cover their faces. The girls were wearing the head scarves to school as a way of saying they felt the Egyptian government was not paying enough attention to traditional religious laws and customs. Egypt's education minister responded by issuing a decree that girls were required to come to public school with their faces bare. The argument has gone to Egypt's courts to decide.[10]

The French government has banned scarves worn by Muslims in its public schools, too, but for a different reason. The French have a tradition of secular education—education that is not based on religion. It does not teach religion and it does not support one religion over another. The French Education Minister felt that girls wearing the scarves caused a separation between Muslims and non-Muslims and, therefore, introduced a religious presence into the schools.[11]

Back in Chapters 4 and 5, we heard the boys' principal argue that he needed to enforce hairstyle rules in order to protect longhaired boys from harassment, to maintain discipline within the school, and to keep students from being distracted from schoolwork. Rules about student appearance are getting even stricter now (in some places, schools are requiring students to wear standard uniforms to school, not just standard-length hair) because the problems caused by student appearance seem to be getting more serious. It has been reported that:

- students have been hurt or killed because robbers wanted the students' clothes. Students have been attacked for jackets, sneakers, gold chains, jewelry, and caps.[12]

- students have been hurt over gang-related clothing.[13]

- students have been upset about having to look at what other students wore. For example, a girl in Ames Middle School in Ames, Iowa, protested a logo worn on some boys' T-shirts that she felt was offensive.[14]

- in some cases, students were paying so much attention to what they were wearing, that they were not paying attention to school. Because students wanted to get enough money to buy expensive clothes, they skipped school, worked too many hours instead of studying, and got involved in illegal activities. Paying too much attention to appearance has also led students to insult each other and to get into fights.[15]

But what about all the lawsuits? Has the law about school hairstyle rules been settled? Not really. The *Tinker* case, the strongest case yet for student freedom of speech, said its rules applied to cases of "pure speech" and did not address hairstyle.[16] Since the boys' case, there have been many hairstyle cases, but with differing results. There have been cases upholding the students and cases upholding the school hairstyle rules. Even when one looks at a particular legal grounds for suit,

There is more variety now in hairstyles. This student's hair is long and short at the same time. He currently attends a public middle school.

one finds differing results. For example, there have been cases that decided that students should not be allowed to bring hairstyle lawsuits under the Civil Rights Act. Other cases, however, have decided that students *can* bring hairstyle lawsuits under the Civil Rights Act.

Even if there were agreement on the rules that should be used, that does not mean that everyone would come to the same result. For example, one of the Supreme Court Justices in the *Tinker* case said he agreed with rules used in that case, but he disagreed with the conclusion—he thought the school should have won.[17]

This is still an area with a lot of room for argument. When those arguments are made, Phil, Paul, and Steve's case keeps coming up, even today, and generally as part of an argument in favor of letting students wear the hairstyles they want.[18]

Finally, even though the Supreme Court did not hear the boys' case, that does not mean that the Supreme Court has ignored students' rights issues. The Supreme Court has, in fact, heard a number of cases in which students' concerns were argued, including

> *West Virginia Board of Education* v. *Barnette* (1943): Upheld student freedom of religion against a public school rule.

> *Tinker* v. *Des Moines* (1969): Explored the issue of students' wearing black armbands in school as a form of speech to protest the Vietnam War.

Goss v. *Lopez* (1975): Held that in order to suspend a student from school, school authorities must let the student know what he or she is being accused of. The student must also be given an opportunity to present his or her side of the story.

Ingraham v. *Wright* (1977): Confirmed that excessive physical punishment of students is illegal.

New Jersey v. *T.L.O.* (1985): Examines the extent to which school officials can search students and students' belongings.

Hazelwood v. *Kuhlmeier* (1988): Examined the extent to which a school principal could delete material from a school newspaper that was written by and intended for students.

Board of Education v. *Mergens* (1990): Held that schools that receive federal funds and allow student clubs must allow students to form their own religious clubs, and must give the religious clubs the same access to school facilities as the other student groups are allowed.

Vernonia School District v. *Acton* (1995): Examined the question of whether a school could do random drug testing on students participating in school athletic programs.

The American legal system is not solely for adults. It also helps clarify and support students' rights.

Questions for Discussion

1. Should a school principal be able to keep students out of school because of their appearance? Why?

2. Should all aspects of appearance be treated in the same way (for example, hairstyle, clothes, accessories, makeup or other forms of body paint, body piercing, neatness/cleanliness, perfume or other body odors) or should some things be treated differently? Should there be rules for some things and not for others?

3. Some rules will only affect school appearance, like clothes. Other rules will affect a student's appearance outside of school, too; for example, you cannot have short hair in school and long hair as soon as you get home. Does this change your answers to question 2? Why?

4. Would it change your answer to question 1 if

    ● students were being hurt by others because of their appearance?

    ● students were being distracted from their studies by concerns about appearance?

    ● students were very offended by what other students wore?

115

5. Should school rules about appearance be very detailed or should they be general and left up to the principal to decide?

6. What if there are rules against long hair for boys but not for girls? Is that discrimination? Support your answer.

7. What if there were rules against long hair for everyone, but some students came from a culture or a religion that required long hair. Would that be discrimination? Support your answer.

8. What if there was something about a student's appearance that led other students to say hurtful things, use bad language, or try to hurt that student? What would you try to do?

9. Should exceptions be made if a student needs an unusual appearance for an after-school job (like the boys in this case, who wanted their hair long so they could be successful rock musicians)? If you would grant an exception, how would you define it? How could you tell the difference between students with an exception and students who were simply breaking the rules?

10. Should exceptions be made if a student's appearance is due to the customs of religion or culture? If you would grant an exception, how would you define it?

11. If you thought your principal did not make good decisions about student appearance, what are some of the things you could do about it?

Chapter Notes

Chapter 1. Hairstyle Keeps Students Out of School

1. *Ferrell* v. *Dallas Independent School District*, Trans., 261 F. Supp. 545 (Tex. 1966) p. 90.

2. Ibid., p. 32.

3. Ibid.

4. Ibid., pp. 23–24.

5. Ibid., p. 547.

6. Transcript of Court Proceedings, Case Number CA-3-1670, p. 203.

7. Ibid., p. 202.

8. Ibid., p. 221.

9. Ibid., pp. 202–203.

10. Ibid.

11. Ibid., pp. 45, 57–58.

12. Ibid., p. 45.

13. Ibid., p. 25.

14. Ibid., p. 59.

15. Ibid.

16. Ibid., p. 245.

17. Ibid., p. 28

Chapter 2. Part of a Bigger Picture

1. *The Jerusalem Bible* 2 Samuel 10:1–11:1; 1 Chronicles 19:1–20:1 (New York: Doubleday & Co., Inc., 1966).

2. Bill Severn, *The Long and Short of It: Five Thousand Years of Fun and Fury Over Hair* (New York: David McKay Company, Inc., 1971), pp. 29, 32, 35, 92–94.

3. Ibid., p. 122.

4. Ibid., pp. 14–15.

5. Jane Duden, *1960s* (New York: Macmillan Publishing Company, 1989), p. 25.

6. 347 U.S. 483 (1954).

7. Edward Grey, *Decades: The Sixties* (Austin, Tex.: Steck-Vaughn Co., 1990), p. 13.

8. Transcript of Court Proceedings, Case Number CA-3-1670, p 223.

Chapter 3. The Boys Go to Court

1. Constitution of the State of Texas, Article VII, Section 1.

2. Vernon's Annotated Texas Civil Statutes, Article 2902.

3. Ibid., Article 2904.

4. 163 U.S. 537 (1896).

5. 347 U.S. 483 (1954).

6. "Suit Talked in Hair Case," *The Dallas Morning News*, September 8, 1996, p. A12.

Chapter 4. The Case for the Boys

All notes for this chapter are taken from: Transcript of Court Proceedings, Case Number CA-3-1670.

Chapter 5. The Case for the Principal

1. Transcript of Court Proceedings, Case Number CA-3-1670, pp. 251–253.

2. Ibid., p. 260.

3. Ibid., p. 262.

4. Ibid., p. 264.

5. *Ferrell* v. *Dallas Independent School District*, 261 F. Supp. 545 (N.D. Tex., 1966), p. 549.

6. Ibid., p. 283.

7. Ibid., pp. 283–284.

8. Ibid., pp. 285–286.

9. Ibid., p. 286.

10. Ibid., p. 289.

11. Ibid.

12. Ibid., p. 291.

13. Ibid., p. 294.

14. Ibid., p. 295.

15. Ibid., p. 301.

16. Ibid., p. 303.

17. Ibid., p. 304.

18. Ibid., pp. 309–310.
19. Ibid., p. 311.
20. Ibid., p. 315.
21. Ibid., p. 318.
22. Ibid., p. 322.
23. Ibid.
24. Ibid., p. 328.
25. Ibid.

Chapter 6. What Happened in Federal District Court?

1. Letter dated September 30, 1966, from the District Court Judge to the attorneys on both sides of the case; Federal Court for the Northern District of Texas, Dallas Division, Case Number CA-3-1670.

2. 347 U.S. 483 (1954).

3. *Ferrell v. Dallas Independent School District*, 261 F. Supp. 545 (N.D. Tex., 1966) p. 551.

4. Ibid., p. 551.
5. Ibid., p. 552.
6. Ibid., pp. 551–552.
7. Ibid., p. 552.
8. Ibid.
9. Ibid.
10. Ibid.
11. Ibid., p. 553.
12. Ibid.

Chapter 7. What Happened in Federal Courts Appeal?

1. John J. Patrick, *The Young Oxford Companion to the Supreme Court* (New York: Oxford University Press, 1994), p. 21.

2. *Ferrell v. Dallas Independent School District*, 392 F.2d 697 (5th Circ., 1968) p. 702.

3. Ibid., p. 704.
4. Ibid., p. 705.
5. Ibid.

Chapter 8. What Happened at the Supreme Court?

1. Petition for a writ of *certiorari*, *Ferrell* v. *Dallas Independent School District* (June 1, 1968), p. 4.

2. *West Virginia Board of Education* v. *Barnette*, 319 U.S. 624, 642 (1943).

Chapter 9. What Happened Next?

1. Transcript of Court Proceedings, Case Number CA-3-1670.

2. Telephone call to Administrative Office of the Dallas Independent School District, November 21, 1996.

3. Ibid.

4. *The Regulation of Student Hairstyles. A Legal Memorandum* (Reston, Va.: National Association of Secondary School Principals, 1969).

5. Bill Severn, *The Long and Short of It: Five Thousand Years of Fun and Fury Over Hair* (New York: David McKay Company, Inc., 1971), p. 132.

6. "Recent Cases on Constitutional Law," *Harvard Law Review*, vol. 84 (May 1971), pp. 1702–1717.

7. 404 U.S. 1042 1046 (1972).

8. 405 U.S. 1032 (1972).

9. John J. Patrick, *The Young Oxford Companion to the Supreme Court* (New York: Oxford University Press, 1994), p. 311.

10. 393 U.S. 503, 511 (1969).

11. Ibid., p. 513.

12. Ibid., pp. 512–513.

13. Ibid., p. 511.

Chapter 10. Where Does This Issue Stand Today?

1. John Fahey and Kristin Gilger, "Students Picket for Long Hair," *Times-Picayune*, December 14, 1989, p. 3B.

2. Douglas Blackmon and Sandra McIntosh, "60 Schoolboys Sent Home for Long Hair," *Atlanta Constitution*, August 29, 1989, p. 1D.

3. Sandra Barbier, "Hair Rule Has Class in Uproar," *Times-Picayune*, May 14, 1994, p. 1BW; Sandra Barbier, "Senior Makes the Cut," *Times-Picayune*, May 19, 1994, p. 1BB.

4. Paul Weingarten, "Texans in a Tangle Over Hair Policies," *Chicago Tribune*, February 17, 1991, p. 1D.

5. Stephanie Asin, "Spring ISD Decides Wigs Will Not Cut It," *Houston Chronicle*, November 9, 1994, p. 25A: Brian Wilkinson, "Growing Dissent: The Politics of Hair," *Seventeen*, May 1990, p. 98.

6. Clay Robinson, "Fighting a Ponytail Not Worth Tax Dollars," *Houston Chronicle*, May 12, 1996, p. 11B; Scott Rothschild, "'90s Hairdo Puts Texan Into Class By Himself," *Boston Globe*, November 21, 1990, p. 3; "Tonsorial Turmoil," *Houston Post*, December 22, 1990, p. 32A.

7. Bob Herbert, "The Valedictorian's Un-graduation," *The New York Times*, June 24, 1995, p. 19.

8. William Curran, "Sauk Village Schools to Trim Hairstyle Policy," *Chicago Tribune*, November 28, 1996, p. C20; "Hair Divides School District," *Chicago Tribune*, November 22, 1996, sec. 1, p. 30.

9. Stephania Davis and Jerry Thomas, "School's Hairdo Ban all Tangled," *Chicago Tribune*, November 12, 1996, p. 1C.

10. Chris Hedges, "In Islam's War, Students Fight on the Front Line," *The New York Times*, October 4, 1994, p. 4A; Vernon Silver, "In Egypt's Schools, Fashion Is Politics," *The New York Times*, June 30, 1996, p. 38.

11. Youssef Ibrahim, "France Bans Muslin Scarf in Its Schools," *The New York Times*, September 11, 1994, p. 4.

12. See for example, Krystal Miller, "School Dress Codes Aim to Discourage Clothing Robberies," *Wall Street Journal*, April 5, 1990, p. 1A; "Your Jacket or Your Life," *U.S. News & World Report*, February 26, 1990, p. 14.; "Robberies Push Detroit's School Board to Propose District-Wide Dress Code," *Jet*, December 25, 1989, p. 29.

13. "School Dress Codes Work," *USA Today*, August 9, 1993, p. 12A.

14. Erin Rollenhagen, "Shirting the Issue," *Seventeen*, October 1994, p. 122.

15. Velma LaPoint, Lillian Holloman, and Sylvan Alleyne, "Dress Codes and Uniforms in Urban Schools," *The Education Digest*, March 1993, pp. 32–34.

16. *Tinker* v. *Des Moines Independent School District* 393 U.S. 503, 508 (1969).

17. Ibid., p. 526.

18. Mary Julia Kuhn, "Student Dress Codes in the Public Schools: Multiple Perspectives in the Courts and Schools on the Same Issues," *Journal of Law & Education*, vol. 25 (Winter 1996), p. 106; Janet Price, Alan Levine, and Eve Cary, *The Rights of Students: The Basic ACLU Guide to a Student's Rights*, 3rd ed., (Carbondale and Edwardsville, Ill.: Southern Illinois University Press, 1988), pp. 41, 44.

Glossary

anarchy—A state of lawless confusion.

arbitrary—Paying no attention to the rules.

capriciously—A decision that is made without real reason or logic.

certiorari—This word comes from Latin and means "to be informed." When the United States Supreme Court wants to hear a case that has been appealed to it, it issues a "writ of *certiorari*" to the court that last decided the case, asking for the case records. To ask the Supreme Court to consider your case, you file a "petition for writ of *certiorari*." If the Supreme Court decides not to hear a case, it "denies *certiorari*" or "denies *cert.*," for short.

correlation—If one thing changes, then the other thing changes; this link is called a correlation. A correlation does not mean that the first change caused the second one, just that the two changes happen together. Principal Lanham testified that there was a correlation between student appearance and student behavior.

cross-examination—The lawyers for each side can take turns questioning witnesses; this gives each side a chance to bring out information important to their side. The lawyer who calls the witness goes first; this is called "direct examination." When he or she is finished, the lawyer for the other side gets to ask questions; this is called "cross-examination." Then, the first lawyer gets to ask questions again; this is called "redirect examination." Finally, the second side gets to ask questions again; this is called "re-cross-examination."

defendant—This is the label used for persons who are being sued, because they "defend" themselves against the charges that they did something illegal.

direct examination—See "cross-examination."

discrimination—Treating people unequally; for example, not letting black students and white students go to the same school. The hard part is deciding when people should be considered equal and when people should be considered unequal. For example, are longhaired and shorthaired students equal? Or are they different in an important way?

minor—A person who is not old enough to be declared an adult under the law.

paramount—More important or the most important.

plaintiff—This is the label used for a person who sues someone else in a civil case.

recess—A break in official court proceedings. As you saw in Chapters 4 and 5, a court can recess for a few minutes or for days.

reconvene—When court proceedings start again after a recess.

re-cross-examination—See "cross-examination."

redirect examination—See "cross-examination."

statute—A law that was passed by state or federal lawmakers.

transcript—A writing that records, word for word, what people said. In this case, the hearing transcript is the written record of what the lawyers, witnesses, and the judge said during the boys' hearing in federal district court.

unenforceable—A contract is "unenforceable" if a court will not hear a lawsuit to "enforce" the contract. In this case, because the boys were minors, the agent could not sue them in court to make them wear the Beatles hairstyle as they promised in their contract. Because the contract did not govern the boys' hairstyle, Judge Taylor did not think the contract governed the result of their lawsuit, either.

Further Reading

Books About Hairstyles and Fashions

Batterberry, Michael, and Ariane Betterberry. *Fashion: The Mirror of History*, 2nd ed. New York: Greenwich House, 1982.

Severn, Bill. *The Long and Short of It: Five Thousand Years of Fun and Fury Over Hair.* New York: David McKay Company, Inc., 1971.

Books About Rock Music

DeCurtis, Anthony, and James Henke with Holly George-Warren. *The Rolling Stone Illustrated History of Rock & Roll*, 3rd ed. New York: Random House, Inc., 1992.

Frame, Pete, et al. *The Harmony Illustrated Encyclopedia of Rock*, 7th ed., consultant editor Mike Clifford. New York: Harmony Books, 1992.

Books About Becoming a Rock Musician

Gelly, David. *The Facts About a Rock Group.* New York: Harmony Books, 1977.

Meigs, James, and Jennifer Stern. *Make Your Own Music Video.* New York: Franklin Watts, 1986.

Meyer, Carolyn. *Rock Band.* New York: Atheneum, 1980.

Books About Civil Rights

Duncan, Alice. *The National Civil Rights Museum Celebrates Everyday People.* United States: BridgeWater Books, 1995.

Goldston, Robert. *The Negro Revolution.* New York: Macmillan, 1968.

Levine, Ellen, ed. *Freedom's Children: Young Civil Rights Activists Tell Their Own Stories.* New York: Avon Books, 1993.

Books About the 1960s

Cleeve, Susan. *Growing Up in the Swinging Sixties.* East Sussex, England: Wayland Publishers Ltd., 1980.

Connikie, Yvonne. *Fashions of a Decade: The 1960s.* New York: Facts on File, Inc., 1990.

Duden, Jane. *1960s.* New York: MacMillan, 1989.

Fisher, Trevor. *Portrait of a Decade: The 1960s.* London: B.T. Batsford Ltd., 1988.

Grey, Edward. *Decades: The Sixties.* Austin, TX: Steck-Vaughn Co., 1990.

Healey, Tim. *The 1960s.* New York: Franklin Watts Inc., 1988.

Hills, Ken. *Take Ten Years: 1960s.* Austin, TX: Steck-Vaughn Company, 1993.

Lane, Joyce. *Our Century: 1960–1970.* Milwaukee: Garth Stevens Publishing, 1993.

Wenborn, Neil. *The U.S.A. A Chronicle in Pictures.* New York: Smithmark Publishers, Inc., 1991.

Books About the Legal System

Friedman, Leon. *Know Your Government: The Supreme Court.* New York: Chelsea House Publishers, 1987.

Goode, Stephen. *The Controversial Court: Supreme Court Influences on American Life.* New York: Julian Messner, 1982.

Patrick, John J. *The Young Oxford Companion to the Supreme Court.* New York: Oxford University Press, 1994.

Books About Freedom of Speech:

Farish, Leah. *Tinker* v. *Des Moines: Student Protest.* Springfield, N.J.: Enslow Publishers, Inc., 1997.

———. *The First Admendment: Freedom of Speech, Religion, and the Press.* Springfield, N.J.: Enslow Publishers, Inc., 1998.

Klinker, Philip A. *The First Amendment.* Englewood Cliffs, N.J.: Silver Burdett Press, Inc., 1991.

Steffens, Bradley. *Free Speech: Identifying Propaganda Techniques.* San Diego: Greenhaven Press, Inc., 1992.

Zeinert, Karen. *Free Speech: From Newspapers to Music Lyrics.* Springfield, N.J.: Enslow Publishers, Inc., 1995.

Index